MINNOWS AND SHOTGUN SHELLS

by Bob Becker

... Northwoods Hunting and Fishing Tales

*With three major illustrations
by Bill Thornley*

Copyright © 2000, Robert J. Becker
Spooner, WI 54801

All rights reserved

No part of this book may be reproduced without written permission from the author.

Printed 2000
In the United States of America
by White Birch Printing, Inc.
Spooner, Wisconsin 54801

ISBN 1-885548-05-2

To order, contact:
Boot Prints
701 College St.
Spooner, WI 54801
Phone (715) 635-2317

Dedication

*To Johnny Walker . . . good friend
and the best walleye fisherman I've known.*

Foreword

For fishermen and hunters, minnows and shotgun shells are basic essentials. Without baits and bullets, not much would take place. Fish wouldn't be caught. Game wouldn't be taken.

Minnows, of course, are but one form of bait. Over some sixty years, I've baited hooks with literally thousands of the scaly critters. All the way from tiny crappie-size to the jumbo northern pike variety... fatheads, shiners, chubs and suckers.

I've fished them alive, and I've fished them dead... examples of the latter being the smelt, ciscos, and bloaters used in my ice fishing. Over time, the minnow has remained the best of all fishing baits, I say.

Close behind, of course, comes the angleworm and night crawler. I've gathered and used my quota of those slimy little beasts also.

Then, to the list can be added a multitude of other natural baits... things like grasshoppers, crickets, cornborers, goldenrod grubs, wood borers, waxworms, crayfish, frogs, mayfly wigglers and dragonfly larva.

Very little that hops, crawls or flutters hasn't at some time been tried as bait by fishermen. Not too many years ago, salamanders were touted as good walleye bait. And an old gent once told me that, as a boy, he'd caught a giant brook trout on a baby mouse.

And their imitations! Since the first line was cast, fishermen have been inventing fake lures. The list is long... plugs, spinners, spoons, plastic worms, hair bugs and feather flies. Pick up any sporting goods catalog, and one can find an almost endless array of shapes, sizes and colors. All intended to outwit a fish!

• • • • • • •

The same with the other essential, ammunition.

The shotgun shell is but one form, having evolved through the centuries since gunpowder was invented. From the musket loads of our pioneer forefathers to the capsulized cartridges we feed into the fancy guns we use today.

Back in boyhood days, shotgun shells were the subject of considerable debate. On back steps, we young hunters would sit to argue the merits of the various brands. Would Super X shells out-shoot Peters High Velocity? Would number six chill shot knock down a pheasant at longer ranges than seven-and-a-halfs?

The outcome was usually a trip to the local Gambles or Sears and Roebuck store for the cheapest shells we could find! The reason being that it took a little doing to scratch up even the 69 cents needed for a box of the low-priced stuff.

Same with rifle shells.

The little .22 caliber rifles we carried back then are collector items today. And we argued at length over cartridges. The shorts sold for only 19 cents for a box of 50. But nobody would admit to using them, though they'd easily topple a cottontail or squirrel.

Yet, that wasn't the point.

A certain amount of prestige and credibility was at stake

with us young bucks. No question, the longs and long-rifle loads were the best. Especially the long-rifle hollow point. Now there was the supreme bullet! And when we could afford the 50 cents for a box, that was what we chose.

To this day, those discussions continue. Especially for high-powered rifle ammo. Is a 180-grain slug superior to a 150-grain? Which is best in brush? Which will shoot flatter in open country?

And from that meditation comes a lot of the enjoyment offered by the sports of hunting and fishing. From thoughts about baits and bullets, from those simple little essentials, come many of our outdoor dreams and fantasies.

Can more walleyes be caught on fathead or sucker minnows? Will low-base shotgun shells loaded with 7 1/2's work well in the modified and improved cylinder barrels of my over-and-under on grouse?

Answers to such questions, of course, lie in the mind's eye of the sportsman. And well they should.

For it is there that the pleasures of hunting and fishing, as sports, truly arise.

Acknowledgements

To recognize and thank all who influenced the words that follow is impossible. For, in truth, that influence extends back over a lifetime, to boyhood days.

To long-gone uncles and grandparents, for example, who helped to spark a love for the outdoors within me.

A grandfather, for instance, who patiently explained how the tiny spruce seeds he'd planted in a coffee can would grow into seedlings, which in time would become part of the windbreak that sheltered his farm home.

And two uncles who fanned my love for fishing by allowing me to share seats with them in flat-bottomed rowboats on Sunday afternoons.

Too, appreciation must go to three very dedicated English teachers in my high school and college years. For from their teachings came a semblance of skill to string words, to express in writing what burned within my brain.

And over time, over more than six decades of adulthood, the multitude of companions with whom I've shared the outdoors. Friends beginning in boyhood times of willow fish poles and slingshots, to senior years of fancy well-equipped boats and scope-mounted rifles.

The list of such folks, most outstanding sportsmen, would extend into the hundreds. And from each came something…

a value, a skill, a perspective… a little something that I could carry away as a treasured memory.

And tribute certainly must be paid to the kind folks who gave me a chance the past 14 years to put my words into print… publishers and editors who allowed me to pursue a crazy dream.

Lastly, my wife, Marian. Without her support and help; no columns, no stories, no books would have come to be. She became a most constructive critic, and I learned to value her judgment.

Yes, I wrote the stories that follow, each and every word of them. But what they say, how they say, and that they exist at all… well, that must be credited to all those fine people who guided my hand along the way.

I'm grateful.

The Author

Contents

SPRING

A River For Boys 3
Trout Streams Are Special 6
Old Dumpy's A Sweetheart 9
Bait Shops Were Wondrous 13
Shaking Hands With A Trout Stream 16
Walleyes From The Wild 19
Cold Water Down The Waders 23
Dancing Sharptails 26
Opening Day Was Different 29
Minnesota Fishin' Camp 33
Big Flop Trout Trip 37
Antique Outboard Motors 40
High Water Trout 44
Shakey From Snakey 47
Leg-Sore and Bug-Bitten 51
Fat-Lipped Muskie 54
The Lady Lifts The Spirit 58

SUMMER

Floating The Namekagon 62
Big Al, My Boat Buddy 66
Summer Trout Miseries 69
Alaska Fishing Guide 72
Ed Robinson...River Guide 75
The Otter Kind of Fishing 79

Hang A Right In Sidnaw 82
Big Al's A Sly Rat 86
Aspen Is Important 90
Terry Brown Teaches Safety 93
Bluegills At Their Best 97

FALL

Acorns Grow Oaks and Deer 102
Wild Boars Are Not Boring 105
Lady Summer Bids Good-Bye 109
My Friend Bill 113
A Hunger For Hunting 117
A Fishing Season Ends 120
A Good Grouse Day For Butch 123
Grouse Keep Getting Sneakier 127
Fall Walleye Memories 130
A Quality Called Courage 133
Deer Hunting Wasn't Lady-Like 137
An Impossible Dream Comes True 140
A Hunter For 65 Years 143
Montana Elk Guide 147
A Half Century of Deer Hunts 151
Deer Seasons and Christmas Trees 154
Grandson's First Deer 157

WINTER

Cottontails and Northern Pike 162
Pity The Poor Chaps 165
A Winter Grouse Hunt 169
Ice Fishing With Katy 172
Big Winnie's Perch 176
Hooked On A Hobby 180
Crappies Shake WInter Doldrums 184
Winter Logging Feeds Deer 187
Fish Science Hall of Famer 191
Putting Winter To Bed 195

Spring –

… The scene was exhilarating, beautiful to spring-hungry eyes. Slowly, Walker eased the boat away from the landing, his oars creating miniature whirlpools that spiraled in the gray water. The soft, rocking roll of the boat felt good; mind-soothing, relaxing, as I tied a yellow jig to my line, and prepared to make my first cast of the season.

Around us, the world was coming to life. From the woods along the shore, a mourning dove cooed its plaintive 'hoo-hoo-hoo'. Overhead a string of migrating bluebill ducks whistled past. In marshy bays, nesting pairs of mallards, the drakes resplendent in their spring plumage, swam and quacked. And from a clump of tall white pines on an island, a bald eagle huge and majestic with snow-white head and tail, flushed at our approach…

A River For Boys

April's a bitter-sweet month, we all know... a mixed-up mess of warm sunshine and wild snowstorms. Calendar-wise, it's a time of adolescence. April can't quite seem to make up its mind as to what it wants to do, or what it wants to be. It's a time when we live on the ragged edge of winter and the rugged edge of spring.

But, most of all, April's a time of birth and awakening, of new life around us and revived spirit within us.

Never were those feelings stronger than in my boyhood!

Let the melting snowbanks send their rivlets of water down the ditches of my country road, let me shed my heavy winter mackinaw, let my feet touch soft bare earth once again, and my heart would lead me to pasture creeks and backwoods ponds, to explore and ponder the secrets of nature.

There I'd lie on my belly and watch crayfish scurry in the rocks of a stream bottom. There, I'd slip off my heavy work shoes and wade barefooted into mucky waters to dip beady strings of frogs' eggs into mason jars borrowed from my mother's basement canning supplies.

As the warmer days of May neared, however, my thoughts would once more stir. With my curiosity staved for the new life bursting around me, satisfied by newly-built nests and

"Minnows and Shotgun Shells"

freshly-dug burrows, a new appetite would begin to burn within me. And my mind would drift to fishing, of rippling water and bullheads and sunfish.

The hunger would grow; and when it no longer could be denied, I'd begin the sharing of my dream with my younger brother, Bill, and my neighborhood buddies. To no surprise, boys being boys, I found that they too felt my yearning. And with heads huddled on back porch steps, we'd plan our first fishing trip of the year.

… to the Pike River.

As rivers go, the Pike wasn't all that much. Maybe thirty feet across at its widest, at no place too deep for us to wade; in the world of rivers, it was at best a lightweight. But to country kids used to jumping puny 'cricks' in cow pastures, it was the mother of all waters. And we revered it, at least for a few of our growing-up years.

And so, an expedition would be organized. Bamboo and willow fish poles were checked. Perhaps a missing fish hook replaced. Maybe a new stringer manufactured from a strong piece of line and a ten-penny nail from the tool shed. And an assumed "blessing" cleared with our folks to be gone for a day from our farm chores.

The trip, you see, would take a full day, the river being some four miles distant. Today, I shake my head in disbelief that our parents would let us kids, youngsters barely eight and ten years old, go off alone on such an adventure. But go we did, and never once did we get into trouble.

Early morning would find the half-dozen of us hiking along the gravel roads north toward the Pike. Over our shoulders, under our arms, and in our pockets were the fish poles, the worm-filled bait cans, and the lunches, usually homemade bread sandwiches, that we'd need for the day.

A River For Boys

The long walk seemed to take forever. But hastened by strong, farm-toughened legs and visions of pools where hungry fish awaited, the miles eventually passed. And finally, that glorious moment when we could plunge down a bank to our favorite rock, unwind our lines, thread on a full-bodied earthworm, and cast out our baited hooks.

There we'd spend the day, watching for a bullhead or a sunfish to jiggle our corks, stolen from old vinegar jugs that grandpa would use for drinking water come haying time.

Ah, but that was living! We never caught many fish. A bullhead or two and a sunfish on a stringer was a good catch. And never big. A six-incher was worth bragging about. Unless, of course, you were lucky enough to tie into a foot-long sucker.

Get your line snagged on a rock or root, and wade out to free the precious hook. No water was too cold to risk losing a hook. And never did scrambled egg sandwiches taste better than eaten on a rock next to moving water, with good-natured boy chatter, ringing through the trees.

Nightfall would find us straggling home... wet, sunburned, shoes muddy, overalls torn, hungry, exhausted, but basking in the glow of a great fishing trip.

Our parents seemed to understand, as I recall.

After all, boys will be boys.

April, 1995

Trout Streams Are Special

Trout dreams about trout streams, that's what's going through my head these days. The long seven-month wait since the season closed last September is about over. Come Saturday, the season will open once more.

Trout streams are special places to me. I can lose the world on a mile of a little lonely creek. Over a lifetime, I've shared a multitude of fishing experiences. But none can top the pleasures I've known clad in my waders, with the power of a stream pushing against my legs, absorbed in a oneness with all that abounds around me.

Those hours come back to life often. As on long winter nights when sleep comes slowly. It's then that I mentally walk my way up the streams I fish. Slowly, casually, in my mind I work myself upstream. Around every bend, through each riffle, past undercut banks where the current swirls deep, where I just know nice browns and brookies lurk.

It's amazing how the character of a stream can become so indelibly etched into one's brain. Push the right button, and like a video tape, the scenario unfolds. And with sound and sensation too. Like the twitter of a red-winged blackbird, the acrid aroma of wet marsh vegetation, and the sting of wind-driven raindrops against one's face.

Why this powerful pull on a person's psyche? The

Trout Streams Are Special

answer's obscure and speculative, of course.

Perhaps it lies deep in our evolutionary past, ingrained there in our make-up when the world of early man was largely one of solitude, broken only by the sounds of natural forces. Wind sighing through treetops, the roar of a waterfall, or the call of an animal in the night. And the muted, subtle sound of his own human voice.

Perhaps that's why today I go to my trout streams. Not just to catch a fish, though ancient man went there too for that reason. But because perhaps I want to re-live those sounds and senses, because I seek not only food for the body, but also food for the soul.

I'm not sure that it's possible to properly describe a trout stream in words. Many times I've tried. Each time I come away feeling that my effort was less than adequate. I've found there's only one way to know, to really know, a trout stream. That's by slipping on a pair of boots and becoming part of it.

And to appreciate the breadth of a stream's full personality, one must traverse it more than once. Some of my streams I've waded dozens of times. On every occasion, a new quirk in its character emerges.

The reason, of course, lies in the fact that the stream is a dynamic entity, constantly shifting and responding to what's going on around it. Water levels rise and fall; beaver dams come and go; trees drop, weaken, and are washed away. All part of the living and breathing of a trout stream.

To know a stream, it must be visited at different times of the day. Never are they better than at dawn when ghostly veils of white mist hang over their valleys, and deer in their red summer coats and gray velvet-colored antlers come to dip their muzzles to drink.

"Minnows and Shotgun Shells"

And at sunset, when the last shafts of sunshine slant surrealistically across the water, blending with the shadows of early evening. A family of coyotes kicks up a chorus in the nearby hills, and a whippoorwill softly calls. Even the most diehard of fishermen will pause to savor such a symphony.

Same for the seasons of the year, even weather fluctuations. A stream in springtime is totally different than in fall. Yellow marsh marigolds and blue violets grow profusely on its banks in June. But the brilliant scarlets and golds of sumac and maple will grace its sides in September.

And a creek suffering in the doldrums of a summer drought, lined with mud flats, can suddenly be transformed into a raging torrent by a three-inch overnight gully washer.

The several trout streams I fish are waiting out there now, flowing black through dead marsh grass and leafless alders. But a few sun-filled days will quickly change all that, sending them bursting with fresh vitality.

And we trout dreamers will be there ... to watch as that wondrous drama of Mother Nature's unfolds.

May, 1995

Old Dumpy's A Sweetheart

I call her Old Dumpy. She's one of my cherished trout streams. I once called her a sweetheart in a story I wrote. And now I say that again.

The first trout outing of this season it would be. Each year it's an agonizing time. I lay awake nights mentally going over the half-dozen streams I fish, analyzing their strong suits, meditating on their weak. Each has something special to offer, and making the decision as to which to fish first becomes a chore. Back and forth I vacillate before I finally make up my mind.

This year it would be Old Dumpy, I decided. And later, I wondered why. As her name implies, she's not the world's greatest trout stream, kind of a klutzy thing that plods her way through marsh grass swamps and alder thickets. Not at all like some of the others that are gifted with rushing rapids and wild, wooded banks.

Why had I chosen Old Dump I kept asking myself, even as I headed the pickup down the backroads toward her. Yet inside me, something, a gut feeling, kept gnawing, telling me "She's the one! Go there!"

I drove over the big culvert through which she flows, turned the truck around, and parked. She looked good, a nice flow of water placidly moving downstream. And my excite-

"A catch of northern Wisconsin brook trout"

ment built as I shuffled into my waders, harnessed my creel to my shoulder, and rigged my rod.

The morning air was cool, a stiff breeze blowing out of the north. My heavy shirt felt good, and I was glad I'd had the sense to slip on some longjohns. Old Dump's water would surely be cold.

Down her bank I inched, picking my way carefully over slippery rocks that marked the water's edge. And I began my fishing, casting my nightcrawler-baited line into swirls and eddys where a trout might hide, waiting there for a tasty breakfast morsel to drift by.

Upstream slowly I moved, working my way around crooks and bends, fighting my way through messes of alders and willows that clawed at my cap and snagged my line as I poked my rod through the tangles. On the banks, caressing Old Dump's face, grew a necklace of yellow marsh marigolds and blue violets. Around me in the air, fluttered a steady parade of birds. Redwinged blackbirds scolded as I invaded their territories. Marsh wrens chattered, and a bevy of spring warblers of different colors flitted through the streamside bushes. A trout stream in spring, I decided, is a beautiful place.

But not a trout, not a bite. Past old haunts I fished, runs and undercut banks where I've caught fish before. Up and over a small beaver dam I crawled. And there at the head of the small flowage where I knew a rock ledge laid underwater, my first fish; a fat brook trout, its gun-metal-blue body beautifully speckled with red and orange dots.

Onward I waded, 200 yards, and another small beaver dam. Through the waist-deep water above it, ever so carefully I picked my way, measuring each step carefully. The bottom was laced with branches and small logs the beavers

"Minnows and Shotgun Shells"

had cut. One misstep would mean a very cold bath.

A second trout, and a third, both fine chunky brookies. Things were looking up. The going was rough, but the fish were there. Within fifty yards I added five to the creel, and the first thoughts of catching a limit crossed my mind. After all, I still had considerable good fishing water ahead of me.

Past old familiar holes and runs I worked, picking up a fish here, another there. And when my mental count of fish caught reached nine, I paused, unbuckled my creel, and laid my catch on a hummock of marsh grass to confirm that number.

The last trout came from the base of a pool where Old Dump's current bumps hard into a bank, sending her water sweeping against the marsh grass. Surely, there a trout would reside. I felt the fish as it picked up my bait, watched as my line angled under the bank, and I set the hook. And shortly the fine brookie came dancing to my hand.

I waded up the bank. There, where the new grass was just beginning to green, I laid out as nice a limit of trout as I've ever caught. Ten brook trout from nine to eleven inches, a matched set.

She's a sweetheart, that old Dumpy!

May, 1994

Bait Shops Were Wondrous

Fishing season opens Saturday, and with it will come considerable scurrying around here in our north country... cottage owners opening their places, cars pulling boats, fishermen checking boat landings.

It's an exciting time, and the odds are good that the majority of the folks will pay a visit or two to a bait shop.

Ah, yes! Bait shops! What wondrous places they were back in younger days when I'd come north with an uncle on a fishing trip. The old-time, old-fashioned bait shop was an institution here in the north, places filled with charm and color all their own. And always operated by friendly, congenial folks who greeted their customers with warmth and enthusiasm.

Cliff and Irelia Peterson, now in their 80's and living in retirement at Angus, remember well the 20 years that they operated a bait shop, Peterson's Minnow Sales, near the south end of Long Lake.

"We started it in 1950," Irelia said. "He got the bait and I sold it!"

"When fishing season opened, I had enough bait in the place so I didn't have to go to the river for a week," Cliff added.

Peterson trapped his own minnows, mainly on the nearby

"Minnows and Shotgun Shells"

Brill and Red Cedar rivers. "But also on some small lakes, where I'd get crappie minnows and fatheads for walleyes," he commented.

"On the Friday afternoon before the opener, the Chicago people coming up to their cottages would begin to arrive," he said. And Irelia added, "We stayed open 24 hours-a-day that weekend. I served coffee and cookies. The season opened at midnight, and usually by two o'clock in the morning, some of them would be out of minnows."

In those days, the bigger shiners and chubs sold for 75 cents to a dollar a dozen. Crappie minnows were six dozen for a dollar, nightcrawlers 35 cents a dozen.

The Petersons lived in a house nearby. The rich loam soil of the area was ideal for nightcrawlers.

"I picked most of the crawlers," Irelia said. "You had to be careful not to rupture them." On the best nights, with Cliff helping, the two would capture up to 4,000. "That place was full of nightcrawlers!" they said.

One night Irelia had to beat a hasty retreat when she shined her flashlight into the eyes of a skunk.

She also dug a lot of angleworms, which were sold as panfish bait. "We sold them 100 to the can," she said. "We never plowed the garden. I dug it all up for worms."

Trapping minnows had its secrets, Cliff explained. "I worked the river for three years before I learned how to trap," he said. "You've got to know where the bait will be in different kinds of weather. I waded the river and used folding wire traps baited with bread. I bought hundreds of loaves of day-old bread."

One day while trapping, he had a close call with a tornado. "In the northwest, there was a darndest-looking cloud. It kept coming closer, and all at once I was looking up right

Bait Shops Were Wondrous

into the eye of a tornado. I pulled my skip (a floating live box) right into the weeds and laid down. It went by right where I'd been."

The Petersons sold tackle too at their shop, buying lures, rods, reels, and other supplies from an Eau Claire wholesale house. Favorite baits of fishermen were Heddon River Runts, Jitterbugs, Flatfish, Blue Tail Fly, and others. Long bamboo cane poles were still popular.

Irelia always had a big raspberry and strawberry patch. "People bought the fruit and the pints of jam I made," she said. "We had a lot of plum trees, and I sold plum jelly... two quarts for two dollars! We also sold maple syrup that we made every spring. And chickens and tulip bulbs!"

"I could sell anything! I even had garage sales. I cleaned out the house! People would ask when I was going to have one."

Serving the public was demanding. "We served lots of nice people," they said. "We had a bell on our driveway. At night when it rang, we'd get up and wait on them. As soon as the yard light came on, the fishermen would start coming."

"When a customer came to our place, the first thing we'd do was visit with them," they said. "We told a lot of people how to take care of their minnows by tempering the water."

Cliff and Irelia Peterson sold their bait shop business in 1970... 26 years ago. Still, the warm relationship they had with the folks they served lingers strong to this day.

"Be sure to say that we enjoyed all the people who came to our shop, and thank them for their business," they asked of me.

With pleasure, Cliff and Irelia... with pleasure.

May, 1996

Shaking Hands With A Trout Stream

I shook hands last week with an old friend… a trout stream. We had a grand reunion.

There's an old adage that says that absence makes the heart grow fonder. Nothing could be more true for me, after a long winter of being away from my trout stream pals.

And why? What makes a trout stream so special?

Well, the answer's easy. At least, for me. My streams, you see, are more than ribbons of water that flow through woods and marshes. For me, they're living entities, critters that breathe and pulsate… creations that have personality, identities that change through the months of spring, summer and fall when I'm with them.

And it's in those quirks of temperament that a bond develops. I know them and how they react, you see, when summer droughts sear their souls, and I know them when three-inch rains recharge their vitalities, causing them to rejoice with laughter.

I've known them as blazing hot suns pierce their pools, and I've known them when soft moonlight bathes their sheltering pines and aspens. And I've shared the multitude of wild things that exist in, on and around their waters; trilliums, red-winged blackbirds, deer, snakes, turtles, dragonflies, and more.

Shaking Hands With A Trout Stream

So it's no wonder then that our reunions are grand.

I parked the truck the other day, sat on the tailgate and slipped on my waders. With trembling fingers I rigged my rod. And finally ready, I cautiously picked my way through the marsh hummocks to the stream's edge to slip into the water.

And my first cast of the season. Well, what should have been a cast. Only the line wouldn't go out. And in disgust, I discovered I'd wrongly threaded my line through a rod ferrule. So, sit down on the marsh grass and do it over! Not an easy task with spider web-thin line and impatience to get fishing.

The stream was in fine shape, not too high nor too low. And with the bankside grass and alders not in leaf, I could pick out every detail of the stream… undercut banks, boulders, submerged logs. Streams change over time, and I made mental notes on how to make my casts in the future.

A hundred yards and the first fish, a six-inch chub. And the first trout, a small brookie that went back into the water.

Ahead laid a deep hole, one of the best on the creek, one that's always good for a fish or two. And from it came two nice keeper brown trout, the largest a good pound-size fish. And around a bend, from under a bank, came another of the same size.

But where were the brook trout, I wondered, as I worked my way upstream. Yellow marsh marigolds garnished the bank, songbirds flitted from bush to bush, their songs of spring filling the air, brightening the day.

And from a run where the stream necked-down between boulders, a keeper brookie, a fat ten-incher, brilliantly speckled with crimson and gold. The fish would prove to be an omen of things to come.

"Minnows and Shotgun Shells"

Casually and cautiously, I fished my way, testing old familiar spots, trying new. The trout weren't exactly jumping into my creel, but the action was good. From runs where the stream's current cut deep against rock-strewn banks came two dandy brooks, fish that pushed a foot in length, heavy-bodied, that fought hard in the cold fast water.

Half-way up the stream, I took a break. I needed one after picking my way around old beaver dams, through boot-sucking mud. And on an old elm that had fallen across the creek, I paused. There I rested, enjoying the scene, the push of the water against my legs. Overhead, not twenty yards above me, passed a pair of Canada geese, happily honking their way to their nesting site.

I finished my wade, caught the rest of my ten-fish limit, and called it a day. Slowly, I hiked my way back to the truck.

Spring was taking command, yet the signs of a winter's passing were still evident… empty milkweed pods; dry goldenrod galls, holes pecked in their sides by birds for the little worms that once lived there; the feathers of a crow that didn't make it.

A winter had come and gone on a trout stream. A new season had arrived. And with it, the pleasure of being privileged to return to extend my greetings.

Every year, about now, that happens.

May, 1998

Walleyes From The Wild

Walleyes in the wilderness, that's what it was. And with a couple of good fishing partners to boot.

The trip had been born in a phone conversation with Johnny Walker, a guy with whom I've spent a fair number of hours on the water. "Bob Speich and I are going to fish the Flowage next week," he'd said. "There's a seat open in the boat if you'd like to come along."

The Flowage, of course, would be the Chippewa Flowage, that 17,000-acre body of water that splotches itself over central Sawyer County, not too far from the back doors of Walker and Speich, both of whom live at Hayward. The two fish the Flowage often. For a couple of reasons. First, because the fishing is usually good. And second, because there's always a quiet corner where a boat can get away from the crowd.

My kind of fishing too!

And a sunny morning a couple days later found us dumping Walker's boat into the water at a secluded landing. Our vehicles would be the only two in the parking lot. Rods, tackle boxes, minnow pails, life preservers were loaded… and across the bay toward a notch in the shoreline Walker headed the boat.

"We marked fish here the last time we were out here,"

"Bob Speich unhooks a nice walleye"

Speich announced, as we entered the narrow neck of water between two pine-covered points. Walker already had that fact on his mind, slowing the boat to study the screen of his fish locater.

But not that day, and along the shore we crept toward big open water ahead. Spring was way ahead of schedule, that was apparent. Quaking aspens were already in full leaf, the bursting buds of the oaks and big-tooth aspen not far behind.

From the debris-strewn shoreline, trees cut by beavers, green-headed mallard drakes flushed. They're bachelors now, enjoying lives of leisure while the hens tend the nests. As we rounded a bend, a deer stood quietly at the water's edge, unperturbed by our passing, its coat rough and ragged, the result of losing its grey winter hair as it changes to its summer red. And high in the branches of a scraggly pine, the white head of an eagle protruded above a thick nest of matted sticks.

"This is where we caught 'em opening day," Walker said, as he eased the boat to a stop and dropped an anchor. "But they were slow, flannel-mouthed." A flannel-mouth walleye to Walker is a fish that picks up the bait, toys with it, but refuses to swallow it.

Such would not be the case this day, however. The fish would prove to be in an aggressive mood.

The three of us would use tiny sixteenth-ounce jig heads, just enough weight to take the minnow-baited hook slowly to the bottom.

And the action began.

On his second cast, Speich tied into a fighter, a northern pike that tried hard to snag itself in a bed of cabbage weeds below. "Mr. Spots," Walker announced, as the fish came into view in the clear water. Mr. Spots would prove to be plentiful, almost a nuisance, as the day progressed. We must have caught 30, all in the one to two pound range, with the exception of one, a five-pounder, which I put into the live well.

But mixed in with the northerns were the walleyes.

Regulations for walleyes on the Flowage call for a three-fish per person daily bag limit with no minimum size. And it became kind of a guessing game to judge whether we had a walleye or a northern on our lines. Normally a northern will make fast runs, while the walleye tends to lug deep, "shaking their heads," as Walker says.

All three of us caught walleyes. Only one was too small to keep, a youthful foot-long fish. And a hefty four-pounder that Speich outwitted proved to be the best. Overall, the walleyes averaged out at about 16 inches, a nice run of fish for our northern Wisconsin waters.

And the wilderness?

Well, that was there too... all around us. During the course of the day, only two other boats passed near enough to notice. Eagles soared overhead, kingfishers darted past, a mink slithered its way through the dead wood along the shore. And the rippling waters of the Flowage made music against a sand bar when we pulled in for our shorelunch.

... A day when a fisherman could feel rich without a nickel in his pocket.

May, 1998

Cold Water Down The Waders

Folks, you should have been there! You should have been there, standing in the woods, watching me wallow and flounder around in that quagmire of a trout stream! You'd have had the laugh of the year!

My first trout fishing excursion of the season, it was. And I was late, more than a week had passed since the season had opened. That's not me! Most years find me on a crick long before that.

Like an obsession, the thought of moving water pushing against my booted legs again, and hungry browns and brookies chomping on the end of my line, had burned in my brain. Finally a free afternoon, and I threw the fishing pole and the waders into the back of the pickup and headed for one of my favorite streams.

Forty-three degrees the thermometer at the bank said as I passed. Cool certainly, almost cold... not the best of trout fishing days to be sure. The saving grace would be the sun that was shining. Perhaps its rays would generate enough warmth to trigger some bug activity in the stream, and thereby turn the fish on, at least a little.

Those were my thoughts, as I parked and slipped into my waders. Maybe the fish would bite, maybe not. Trout fishing, after all, is as much about being on a stream as it is

"Minnows and Shotgun Shells"

about catching fish. Streams have personality, and in time they become close friends.

A ten-minute hike along a woods trail, and at the crest of the ridge, I paused. There, below me, was my old pal, the Beautiful Lady... as pretty as ever, the sun shining on her face, yellow marsh marigolds adorning her banks.

Foot prints in the mud told me that someone else has also paid her a visit. But not this day. Today, I alone would fish her waters... fishing at its finest, without a doubt. For trout fishing is a solitary sport, best appreciated with only the wonders of wild things for company.

And I began my casting. The water is low and crystal clear. Pebbles and yellow sand glisten on the Lady's bottom. Cautiously, I skirt a deep hole to position myself at the downstream end. And the first trout, a keeper brookie, one that liked the looks of a fresh nightcrawler floating past.

But that's all, and I move on to a second hole that has always been kind to me. On the first cast, a fish takes my bait, running with it into a submerged tree branch where it snags the line. That's it. Nobody else is home today, and I move on.

Upstream, I know the Lady narrows, twisting and turning as she passes through marshy terrain. Perhaps there, I'll do better.

From under an overhanging alder, a nice ten-inch brookie, its blue-black sides speckled with orange and gold and violet, comes to the creel. And I slip slowly upstream against the current to where a fast run curls around a downed tree.

The trout hit almost as soon as the crawler landed in the water. At the set of the hook, I knew it was better than average. And as I played it, I turned to slide it up on the grassy bank.

And that's when the bottom dropped out of the creek! Down, my feet began to sink in sticky black goo. Try as I

Cold Water Down The Waders

might, I could not pull them free. And with the muck sucking at my legs, and the current pushing me backwards, over I went!

Well, needless to say a couple of buckets of cold water down the back of one's waders is a thrilling experience! There I laid flat on my back, thrashing in the mud and water, struggling to get back on my feet.

I finally did, and crawled up on the bank. One look at myself, wet from top to bottom, and all I could do was laugh. But my second thought was, "Boy, if anyone had seen that, they'd be splitting their sides!"

Out in the crick, my fish pole laid, and on the bottom, drifting slowly downstream, was my precious supply of nightcrawlers. And into the water again I waded to retrieve as many as I could. Finally, I got to the rod, lifted it, and to my surprise, my trout was still on the line, a dandy foot-long brookie.

The rest of the afternoon was anti-climactic. As cold as it was, and as wet as I was, I really wasn't all that uncomfortable. I finished my wade back to the truck as leisurely as I always do, and I caught some more trout, enough to bring my catch to eight for the day.

Not too bad for the first trout trip of the year... a trip that will be remembered as the time I took a darn good dunking.

May, 1997

NOTICE
WATCH YOUR STEP

Dancing Sharptails

Silently, stealthily, dawn came creeping across the wild back country. Treetops that had stood black against the night sky, were changing to gray, as the first light of daybreak filtered slowly across the forested landscape.

And Bill Thornley and I were lost. Well, at least we'd lost our leader, Bob Dreis. Dreis, a retired wildlife biologist, had invited the two of us to join him on a bird watching trip... sharptail grouse, that these days are in the midst of their courtship dancing on DNR's Namekagon Barrens Wildlife Management project west of Minong.

But somewhere on one of the twisting sand roads, Dreis had made a sharp turn, one where the red tail lights of his car had disappeared, leaving Thornley and me guessing. And for an hour, in pitch-black darkness, we'd driven in vain trying to get re-connected.

And with dawn breaking, just as we were about to give up and head home, Dreis pulled in behind us. "Sorry about that turn," he said. "But if we hurry, I can still sneak you into a blind where you should see some birds."

Fifteen minutes later, found Dreis pointing to a small canvas-covered blind set out in an area of low brush. "You'll probably flush the birds off the dancing ground as you go in," he said in hushed voice. "But they'll come back."

Dancing Sharptails

And a few minutes later, Thornley and I were hunkered cozily inside the four-foot-square, four-foot-high blind. In three of the canvas walls, small portholes had been slit, and from there we planned to aim our cameras... if the birds appeared.

Within a half-hour, they did. Quietly we'd sat on our little stools, listening to the birds calling in the distance. Gradually, their calls grew closer, and then suddenly, there the grouse were, a dozen of them in front of us.

And the sight was spectacular, as they went about their spring mating ritual... wings outstretched, tail feathers fanned, strutting, cooing, clucking. The courtship begins in March and extends to June, with the birds using the same plot of earth, called a dancing ground, over and over.

For a short hour, Thornley and I watched. And when we crawled out of the blind, 17 of the birds flushed, winging their way across the brushy terrain.

Later I visited with Gary Dunsmoor, a DNR wildlife technician who helps to manage the Namekagon Barrens project.

Wisconsin has three species of grouse, he explained: ruffed, sharptail and prairie chicken. "The ruffed is a bird of the forest," he said. "And the prairie chicken is a bird of the true grass prairie. But the sharptail is a bird of the brush prairie."

And that is the way the DNR Namekagon Barrens project is managed.

"The project contains about 5,000 acres, which we lease from Burnett County," Dunsmoor said. "We manage it by controlled burning. Fire sets the vegetation back to shrubs and grass. We burn an average of about 800 acres a year. But we probably won't do any this year. It's too dry."

Historically, Wisconsin's sharptail population peaked in

"Minnows and Shotgun Shells"

the 1930-1940 era. Clear-cutting of the virgin timber followed by frequent fires created an open brushy landscape. Add in a myriad of small backwoods farms that served as food patches, and ideal sharptail habitat existed.

But with time, as protection from wild fires became effective, and as agriculture faded and open lands were planted to trees, the habitat changed, and the bird declined. Today, while small flocks still exist elsewhere, most of the birds are found on managed areas.

The Namekagon Barrens project has a fall population of about 200-300 birds, Dunsmoor said. While the season was closed to hunting in 1996, he's optimistic that hunting of the bird will again be allowed this fall. Surveys that are planned will determine a quota of birds that could be taken without over-harvesting the population.

There was a time when sharptail grouse hunting in northern Wisconsin was big sport. Old-timers still talk about those days. One, my late long-time friend Ken Wallin, formerly of Grantsburg, once sent me an account of the great hunting that he and his friends enjoyed years back in the sand barrens region.

Can those days return? Not likely, but the bird's presence can be maintained, and with it, a carefully controlled semblance of the past sport.

And the aesthetics of the bird, the thrill of seeing them! As Dunsmoor put it, observing their courtship dancing is one of the most unique things in nature.

"Many people are using the blinds," he said. "Anyone interested in doing so, should give me a call."

Being there is a rare outdoor treat... I speak from experience.

April, 1997

Opening Day Was Different

Folks who fish trout know that conditions vary a lot over the course of a season. The character of the streams change, not to mention the habits of the fish themselves.

Our recent opening day was a good example.

Normally on the opener, I'm clad in extra-warm clothes, usually longjohns, to protect against both cold air and cold water.

Not this year. I broke a sweat just getting into my waders! One look at the cloudless blue sky, the bright sun climbing over the eastern horizon, the leafless trees, and I knew I was in for a different kind of a day.

"It's going to be a hot one!" I said to myself, as I picked my way down the bank and cautiously slipped into the water. I'd be fishing Old Dumpy, a stream that's been a friend of mine for many years.

And it suddenly dawned on me that perhaps I'd made a poor choice. Old Dumpy is a lazy stream, one that meanders its way through a flat swamp; terrain that offers very little shade to the water... at least until the marsh grass grows up to shield her banks.

Perhaps I should have gone somewhere else, to a stream that flows through wooded hills, where the sun wouldn't be beating directly down on the water... as it was already doing

"An opening day bag of brooks and browns"

Opening Day Was Different

on Old Dumpy.

Trout fishermen learn that bright sunlight makes for poor fishing.

But no time for second guessing! I'd fish Old Dump for better or for worse!

And a quick, pleasant surprise. From under an overhanging bank, a foot-long brookie darted to grab my nightcrawler. A quick hook set, and I thought the fish was mine. But some rusty fishing technique! A careless loop of slack line, and the trout wrapped itself around a root, to pull free.

Encouragement, however. Perhaps the fish were feeding... which would offset the tough fishing conditions.

On upstream, to a pool that's always good for a fish. It was. In fact two, nice keepers, a brown and a brook. The creel wouldn't be empty!

The wade around a long bend and through an old beaver pond produced nothing. But then, my favorite spot on the creek, a rocky run that flows deep and swift. From it came two more, a brookie and a brown. And a pool below the remains of a rotting beaver dam yielded yet another.

Things weren't looking too bad! Five fish, half a limit, rested in the creel... even with the rugged fishing conditions!

And that's when I heard the cough!

Now, it's rare for me to see another fisherman on Old Dumpy. Especially one plodding through the tangle along her banks. That's very tough going. Yet, there he was.

What to do? Get out of the stream and go elsewhere, I decided. And back to the truck I hiked.

I'd take a look at a section of stream down the road a mile or so. Perhaps no one would be on it. And as luck would have it, the parking area was empty.

I parked, gathered up my gear, and began my hike. I'd

"Minnows and Shotgun Shells"

walk downstream a couple hundred yards, hit the creek, and fish it back to the truck. Maybe I'd add a fish or two to my catch, enough to make for a tasty supper.

High noon was approaching as I stepped into the stream. What with the hot sun and the hike, beads of sweat dripped down my neck. As I'd done several times earlier, again I dipped my cap into the cold water to cool myself.

Steathily, I sneaked my way to the base of a run where the current undercuts a bank. And on my second cast, a dandy brown, a fish that fought hard in the swift water.

Around a bend to an old familiar hole. And from its rocky bottom came a respectable brook trout.

The action was better than I expected! And I paused for a rest, to sit on a large boulder in the middle of the creek… to let the stream swirl and gurgle about my booted feet. Yellow marsh marigolds dotted the bank. Overhead a brilliantly feathered drake wood duck passed, and in the distance a woodpecker hammered out a melody on a dead tree trunk. Trout streams can be truly beautiful places!

And with renewed enthusiasm, I moved on. Three more trout soon came to the creel, an opening day limit.

I'd worked hard, and I'd had to adjust to some tough fishing conditions, plus some competition.

But then, what else is new in the trout fishing business!

Each trip is different. That's what makes them so memorable.

May, 1999

Minnesota Fishin' Camp

So what if the ketchup squeezed out of a yellow jug made for mustard!

And my snoring? So what if I'm world class!

Such was life recently in a lonely backwoods fishing camp tucked in the wilds of northern Minnesota. Four of us, long-time members of the perch fishing gang that I hang around with, gathered there recently… Al Spindler from Eau Claire, Joe Zanter of Sparta, Bruce Moss, a Spoonerite, and myself.

The trip hadn't been easy to organize. Back in my prime, the words of an old song once said, "Wedding bells are breaking up that old gang of mine!" Well, now it's old age. Everybody's tied up with the complications that go with being a senior citizen. Things like kids and grandkids coming, doctor appointments, and social obligations.

But after a couple of weeks of negotiation and compromise, much by long-distance telephone, a plan was finally made. And an early morning last week found the four of us heading north toward Duluth and points beyond, dragging boats behind our vehicles loaded with fishing gear, groceries and other essentials we'd need for our stay.

Our destination would be Ball Club Lake near Deer River. The big oval-shaped body of water, we've found, holds a large population of yellow perch that run up to a foot long, not to mention northern pike that almost become pests, and a respectable stock of walleyes. Wild and beautiful, the lake is rimmed with natural northwoods scenery; trees, marshes and bulrush beds.

And tucked into that setting, lies the Ball Club Lake Lodge, our home away from home when we come to fish. There, in a comfortable cabin, appropriately named "Deer", only a stone's throw from the boat harbor, we holed up.

Talk about getting away from it all! We did. Just ourselves; Jon and Marion Mason, who run the place, and their youngsters; and a handful of other early-season fisherpeople, men and women, like us, who'd come to relax and recreate.

And the fishing!

Well, it was excellent. I've never seen the perch bite more aggressively. Our group set a nine-inch minimum size on the fish we'd keep. And we had no problem finding fish above that.

Bruce Moss fished with me in my boat. He's an excellent angler, observant and quick to adapt to the whims of fish. We found the perch schooled in shallow water up tight against the bulrushes. There, as Moss noticed, they were feeding on mayflies that were hatching. The flies were emerging from the mud of the lake bottom, and as the nymphs rose to the water's surface, the perch were taking them.

Using light spinning tackle, we caught fish both on "cut bait", minnow halves, and artificial lures. At one point, the fish were in such a feeding frenzy that we switched to small strips of white pork rind, which worked just fine.

Mixed with the perch were the ever-present northern pike. We landed and released many, and we lost a lot more as the fish cut our lines with their sharp teeth.

Minnesota Fishin' Camp

The last day of our stay, Moss and I loaded the boat and moved to Cut Foot Sioux Lake, an extension of Big Winnibigoshish, to try for walleyes. The walleyes move into Cut Foot to spawn, then slowly drift back to the big lake. Casting jigs, we caught three in a morning shortened by a road under construction and a strong wind.

Wind was a problem throughout our stay. Over time I've learned to always bring a second anchor along. But at times, even with two anchors out, we had trouble keeping the boat where we wanted it.

And it was cold, a drastic departure from the El Nino warm weather we've been having all spring. The longjohn bottoms I'd thrown in my duffel bag at the last minute sure felt good.

But throughout it all was the fun, the losing of oneself on a wilderness vacation. Good companionship, good hosts... little things like the plateful of tasty breakfast muffins that Marion Mason baked and brought over. And Nick, their fifth-grader son, who came by the fish-cleaning house twice to help with the job of filleting our catches. And then thanking US for letting him help!

So what if Zanter's ketchup was in a mustard jug!

And in no way will I ever believe that I snore THAT loud!

June, 1998

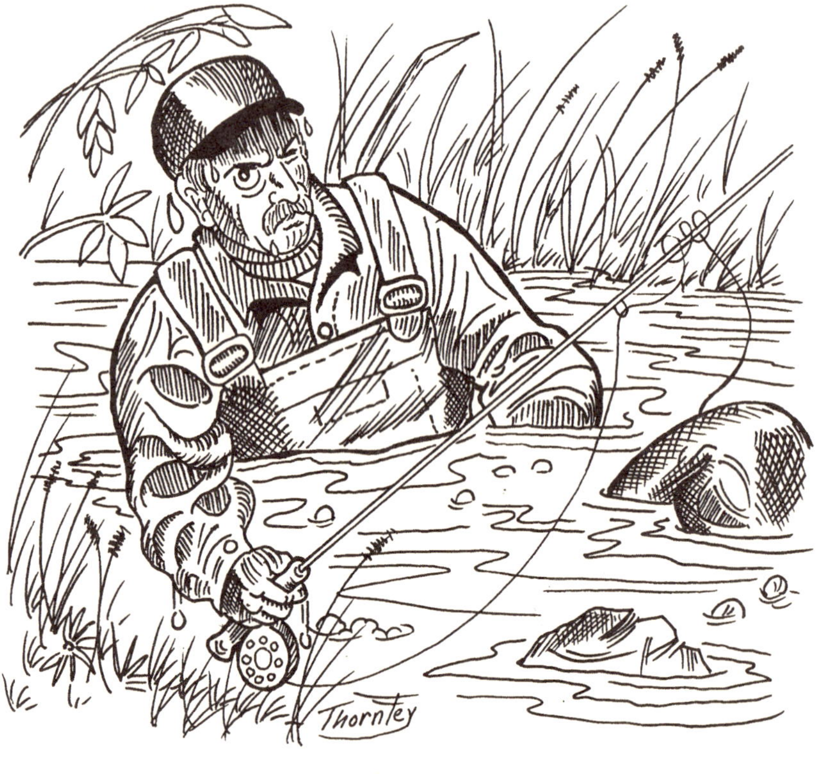
Thornley

Big Flop Trout Trip

Can a trout fishing trip be a big flop, yet at the same time, a huge success?

Yes, I say. I know because that's how it happened the other day on one of my favorite streams, the one that I call The Beautiful Lady.

The day had begun innocently enough. I'd parked the truck in my usual place, slipped into my waders, snapped on my creel, and with fishing rod in hand, started up the trail I walk to reach the Lady.

The quarter-mile hike, for some reason, seemed to require more exertion than in past years. Maybe the hill had grown steeper over winter, I speculated. Or perhaps I was out of shape from too much soft living. Naw, it couldn't be that, I told myself.

Finally, puffing and wheezing, I reached the top of the ridge, where the trail begins its descent into the valley where the Lady flows. There she was, crystal clear, freshly scrubbed by a recent rain, all squeaky clean after her long winter nap.

Ah, but isn't she beautiful, I thought, as I caught my first sight of her, her water rippling over a rocky riffle. Then, halfway down her slope, I heard her voice, the music she makes as she flows, lyrics she's played for thousands of years, notes that fishermen like me come to enjoy and cherish.

I reached her side and slowly stepped into her current, its caress pushing against my booted feet. Slowly, cautiously, I waded my way downstream, to where her bank is less steep. There I'd again walk her shore, down to the thick swamp through which she passes, to where I'd begin my fishing.

Past an old beaver dam and an abandoned lodge of mud and sticks. Under big popples that the animals once cut, where I crawl on my hands and knees. And finally, to a large pool where I'd make my first cast.

Carefully, quietly, I wade into position. And the tap-tap of the first fish mouthing my nightcrawler-baited line. I set the hook, and a nice brook trout comes dancing out of the water. Ice-cold, it feels to my hand, as I pick it from the water and drop it into my creel.

A few steps further into the pool I move, and resume my casting. Another trout is waiting, this time a chunky footlong brown that flashes silver and bronze as I play it in the clear water.

And shortly, another, one that's almost a twin. Three trout from the pool! The Lady is being kind today, I say to myself. And I move on upstream.

A hundred yards of shallow runs produce nothing, and I begin my wade around a rocky riffle cluttered with rotting brush and sticks.

And there is where the trip turned into one big flop!

I know I'm not the most graceful person in the world. Being somewhat heavy on the top side, I figure my center of gravity is precariously perched about at my Adam's apple. Every year I dunk myself in a trout stream at least once! It's inevitable!

Big Flop Trout Trip

Oh, it must have been a sight to see! The Lady must have certainly chuckled. One minute I'm on my feet. The next, my right leg is headed north... my left leg south... my left arm, holding my fishing rod, west... and my right arm is gyrating over my head!

Fortunately the stream was only a few inches deep, and I didn't take on too much water. But as I rose to my feet, there was my bait box hanging empty, it's cover askew. Gone was my precious supply of night crawlers!

Well, after addressing myself in some not-so-polite-terms, and cooling my head, I decided I'd go to Plan B, my contingency plan for such circumstances. I'd fish the rest of the stream with spinner baits. I really didn't have much confidence. Artificial lures usually don't work too well early in the season, especially when the water is extremely cold.

But I really had no choice! What the heck, I could still enjoy The Beautiful Lady. I'd check out her pools and undercut banks to see what changes she'd made over winter.

And that I did. And to my surprise, in the process I landed four more nice trout, three browns and a brookie. My creel had some heft to it when finally, leg-weary, I reached the truck once more.

The trip had gone from a big flop to one I'd long remember.

The way I figure it, the Lady must have felt sorry for me... nice gal that she is!

May, 1995

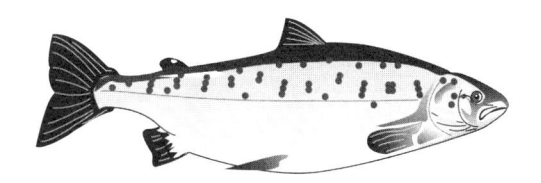

Antique Outboard Motors

Almost a hundred years of northern Wisconsin history rests in a shed at Don Harper's home in Minong. Harper is a collector of old outboard motors. At the present time, he owns some 430, motors that date back to the turn of the century.

There the antiques reside, many standing side-by-side on the floor, others hanging from the walls and rafters. There they stand, the aluminum castings of the true oldies still shining brightly, the once-fresh paint of others now softly fading with time.

And over all, hangs an aura of days gone by... when people first came here to our north country, to its lakes and rivers, to fish and to recreate.

Listen to Don Harper talk about his prizes, and it's apparent that he's an authority, an expert, on outboard motors. He speaks fluently about both the old and the new... their origins, histories and inner-workings.

And rightly so. He's spent a lifetime, you see, around outboards.

"My folks owned a resort east of Hayward, and my dad repaired motors," Don said. "He started me tearing motors down in 1948. Then I went to Korea. When I came home, I started a little backyard shop of my own. I was an Evinrude

"Don Harper collects old outboard motors"

"Minnows and Shotgun Shells"

dealer in Hayward from 1957 to 1976. Then I sold out and moved to Minong to work for Bob Link.

"Collecting old outboard motors is easy. They're so cheap. There's lots of them sitting in garages, and nobody knows how to fix them. Many are nostalgic motors that grandfathers once used!"

"When I came here, I had two motors," he continued. One was a 1928 Model A35 Johnson. Mary Ellen, my wife, and I still use it to fish for bluegills on some of the little lakes around here."

"Mary Ellen is a very helpful partner. She answers a lot of phone calls, and she goes with me to collector shows. And she's found some of the motors herself at garage sales!"

Harper has donated two motors to the Fishing Hall of Fame at Hayward. "One was a 1911 Evinrude, and the other was a 1924 ELTO. Both were made by Ole Evinrude at Milwaukee."

Evinrude was a pioneer inventor and manufacturer of outboard motors.

"When I first decided to collect motors, people found out, and they gave me all kinds of them," Harper commented. "One day a man stopped here at the house to ask about motor values. His dad had left him 30. When he got back to Chicago, he mailed me a list of them. The next day, we drove to Chicago, and I bought 18 from him!

"Then I got interested in certain models. Some makes didn't run good, and only a few were made. Those oddballs are the most valuable!"

"When I retired, I intended to restore them. But now people keep bringing in their present-day motors for repairs, and I don't have time to work on the old ones!"

Harper belongs to the Antique Outboard Motor Club, a

Antique Outboard Motors

national organization of about 3,000 members. "Each state has at least one club," he said. "Anyone interested in the organization may contact me."

The group sponsors shows and meets for collectors. "There'll be a big international meet at Tomahawk, August 4 to 7. I'm going to one at Horicon April 25. I'll take about 50 motors along and try to sell some."

Motors of the past were far different than today's... small, portable, with rope starters and built-in gas tanks. "Everybody carried a gallon of gas along in the boat," Don said.

"This is a 1.7 horsepower Clark Troller," he said, holding a beautifully-crafted small motor. "You had to wrap the rope around the prop to start it. I found it in a salvage yard at Turtle Lake."

And a 1/2 horsepower Evinrude Mate. "It's a little dinky 'martini mixer'!" he noted.

Harper has three rules for good care of modern-day outboards. "One, keep the lower unit gear case full of clean oil. Two, watch the water pump. You can't start a motor dry anymore. And three, bleed the gas line from the tank after the motor's been unused for a time."

Harper plans to sell some of his motors. "I've got way too many," he said. "Maybe other people will be interested in some for their own collections."

Parting with some of his prizes may not be easy, however. Memories of his years of collecting may linger strong.

"It's been a lot of fun," he said, recalling those years.

April, 1999

High Water Trout

Hey! I finally caught some fish!

It's about time, you say? Hey, I couldn't agree more! I'm off to a rough start, to say the least, this year.

A day of free time finally had worked it's way into the calendar. That's where the story begins. Finished were the several spring projects that had taken on high priorities, duties like planting trees and getting the yard in shape. Duties performed, however, with a certain amount of daydreaming about what might be happening out on the trout cricks.

And those thoughts came into sharp focus as I gathered up my gear; rod, creel, waders, my fishing vest and a bait box of nightcrawlers. In the course of a summer, I fish several streams, and it's always kind of a juggling act to decide which one to try.

I'd fish Old Dumpy, I decided. As trout streams go, she's nothing fancy. Fish her, and you soon learn why. You'll find no rushing rapids, no classic trout creek characteristics. Just a stream plodding its way, twisting and turning as she muddles her path through the alder swamps.

But this time of the year, early spring when her water's cold, sometimes she produces some fine brook trout. And fine brook trout are dear to my trout fishing heart.

High Water Trout

Enter another factor into the picture, however... a rainstorm.

As I drove up to Old Dump, one look told me that she was unfishable. Obviously, I'd underestimated the amount of rain that a series of thunderstorms had dropped two nights before. There she was, out of her banks, the meadow through which she flows, flooded. No way could she be fished.

What to do? And my brain wheels began to spin to come up with a second choice.

I'd head over to my Beautiful Lady friend. Sure, she'd been very inhospitable the time I'd fished her on opening weekend. But she'd be fishable I figured, at least a stretch where her high banks would contain the high water.

Now normally I like to fish trout when the water's high. But there's a limit! And that became abundantly clear when I reached the Lady's edge. There she was, just a-roaring; a side of her personality that's a pleasure to see and hear, but one where you'd better be sure of your footing as you wade. A slight misstep, a slight loss of balance, and she'll take your feet right out from under you!

Fishing a stream under those conditions is a special experience. You quickly realize that it's a case of you and the river. You're all alone with the water's power, and if you get into trouble, well, you're on your own to get out of it.

Slowly I picked my way downstream, along the bank, over and under trees cut by beavers, to where I began my fishing... at a deep run once guarded by a giant spruce tree, now dead from past beaver flooding.

Upstream against the current, I moved. Fifty yards, and the first fish, a ten-inch brown trout that goes into the creel. Never throw back the first keeper, I say, an old bad-luck superstition of mine.

"Minnows and Shotgun Shells"

Onward I moved, reading the stream's bottom carefully with my feet. The swift current had done some re-arranging, soft sand sucking at my boots in places.

My second fish came from a pool below the site of an old logging dam. At the set of the hook, I knew it was a fine fish. Around the pool it raced, splashing airborne in a jump. With care I played it, finally bringing it to my hand, a thirteen-inch, pound-plus brown. And I pause to admire its silver, orange-dotted sides, marvelling how a small stream can produce such a fine fish.

A hundred yards I wade. Through a rock-strewn rapids where last year I went on my back-side in the slippery boulders. Now with the torrent of water, it's particularly tricky.

From a deep run above, came my last two fish, both foot-long beauties. One was a full-bodied brook trout, a fish with gun-metal blue, violet-spotted sides; the other a chunky brown.

That was it! I fished the rest of the Lady's way, up to a flooded meadow that I'd have had to swim to fish. And I packed it in. I'd had enough. Legs tired from fighting the strong current told me so.

Once again, the Lady had been kind. Her disposition had improved, as I knew it would.

She'd finally yielded a few fish.

June, 1996

Shakey From Snakey

Spend time in the outdoors and it's a good bet that something new will pop up with wildlife. Like the other day, when Johnny Walker and I were fishing, and a big snake tried to climb into our boat.

But more about the critter later. First, the fishing.

Walker and I had gone to the Chippewa Flowage over in Sawyer County to try our luck on the walleyes. Walker, retired guide that he is, had done some exploring a couple of trips earlier and had found a hot spot.

That's what's nice about fishing with old guides. They usually know what they're doing when they hit the water.

The four-mile run from the landing was sheer pleasure… around islands, through narrow necks of water, along floating bogs, past a huge white pine with an eagle nest in its crown. Green-headed mallard drakes swam lazily in sheltered coves. They're bachelors now. The hens are back home tending nests.

And finally, Walker eased his boat up to a steep shoreline cluttered with aspen trees that beavers had clear-cut, the tops of which laid in the water… perfect fish cover.

And, as old guides are supposed to do, Walker showed the way. On his first cast, he hooked a scrappy northern pike. The fish, too small to keep, was released. But it proved to be

"John Walker and a Chippewa Flowage walleye"

Shakey From Snakey

a harbinger of things to come. Before our day would end, we would catch a couple dozen at least, the largest a five-pounder.

But it was walleyes that we were after.

"We didn't do much on them until afternoon the last time I was here," Walker said.

We fished leisurely, casting small jig heads tipped with minnows to the edges of the "wood" that littered the shore. Snagged lines and lost jigs were common, something one has to expect if he's going to fish such water.

And finally, a start on the walleyes, as Walker landed a pound-and-a-half 14-incher. "Not the biggest," he said, "but it'll do!"

"Never throw the first keeper back," I answered. "That's bad luck!"

And another handicap as the weather warmed. White "popple fuzz" began to blow about. The fuzz, really seeds of aspen trees, floats on the water, where it collects on fishing lines, making casting more erratic.

Periodically, Walker would move the boat a short distance to try new water. The northern pike seemed to be everywhere. We landed many and had lines cut by more.

But the walleyes proved to be finicky. Still, by noon, when we pulled up to a sheltered, pine-covered point for lunch, four swam in the boat's live well, two-thirds of our six-fish limit. Not too bad!

A half-hour for sandwiches and coffee, and back on the water for the last two.

And that's when the snake paid us a visit! I saw the critter, a five-foot long pine snake, as it entered the water at the shoreline.

"There's a snake out there, Johnny!" I said pointing. "And

"Minnows and Shotgun Shells"

it's heading right for us!"

And it was! The snake must have figured the boat was something it could crawl up onto, maybe take a sunbath. Because it never wavered! Right to us it came, it's head out of the water, it's long brown-and-black body undulating as it swam.

Right to the side of the boat, directly in front of me it came! I was certain it was going to come right over the side into my lap! And I grabbed a boat cushion and gave the side of the boat a couple of good swats.

In the rear, Walker was standing, swinging the landing net! Neither of us wanted any part of the beast.

Our efforts paid off. Suddenly the snake appeared on the opposite side of the boat, to continue on its way toward a distant shore.

"That's a first for me!" I said to Walker. "I've had them swim past me in trout streams but never like this on a lake."

"They're harmless," Walker responded. "They live mostly on mice!"

And with that the Old Guide and I went back to catching our final two walleyes!

I, a bit shakey from snakey, however.

May, 1999

Leg-Sore and Bug-Bitten

My longtime trout stream pal, Old Dumpy, is a temperamental, irascible thing... sort of the Ma Kettle of trout streams, I'd say.

Not that it's all her fault. I blame her disposition on the way she's been forced to live. Who's to say what kind of personalities any of us would have, were we forced to live in a dismal, demeaning swamp our entire existence!

No wonder she doesn't give a you-know-what about her appearance, that she's disheveled and rundown at the heels. I'd be too, if I had to constantly fight off alder brush clogging my nostrils and beavers plugging my arteries!

Sure she's on the touchy, somewhat cranky side. But she's good-hearted, I've found! She'll give a fisherman the shirt off her riffles if you give her a chance!

I found that out the other day.

All spring she'd been on my mind. Every year it's the same. I look forward to fishing her. But never really knowing what to expect. At times I've come away with catches of brooks and browns that will never fade from my memory. Then at other times, I've left her with nothing more than two weary, aching legs.

Those were my thoughts the other afternoon as I stepped into her water. Take my time, enjoy my wade along her

"Minnows and Shotgun Shells"

twisting, turning banks. Enjoy it, that is, as much as it's possible what with her muck and mire.

Maybe I'd catch a fish. Maybe I wouldn't. My pleasure would come from being there, from seeing how perhaps she'd changed, how she'd fared through the winter.

Overhead hung a mostly cloudy sky, broken only occasionally by a swatch of blue. Not a bad day for fishing, I thought, as I began casting my nightcrawlers into her current.

Upstream I worked, perhaps a couple hundred yards, with no trout action, pestered only by chubs and horned dace. And I found myself wondering if that would be the rule for the day. Maybe Old Dump was in one of her grumpy moods.

Etched in my mind was a thick file of memories of fish caught in the past, of undercut banks and sharp bends where the current cuts deep. Special places where my anticipation runs high. Like the hole ahead where once I'd taken a foot-and-a-half-long brown, the water exploding as the fish leaped, silhouetted in silver against the green marsh grass.

Twice, three times, I drifted my crawler through the hole. And then, the soft tap of a feeding fish. Another chub, I figured, as I raised my rod.

No chub, I soon learned. Around the hole the fish fought, and finally I skidded it onto the bank, a handsome 13-inch brown. A fine fish, one that would make the rest of the afternoon almost anti-climactic.

On I continued, past an old beaver dam, through the mud of its former flowage. And above, where Old Dump narrowed between marshy banks, another fine brown trout, almost a twin to my first. And a smaller brookie to add to my creel.

Ahead laid my favorite stretch of water, perhaps 60 feet of

Leg-Sore and Bug-Bitten

high bank where boulders lie strewn in the stream. Like a stalking blue heron, I cautiously positioned myself at the toe of the run and began my casts.

Almost at my feet, the fish hit, so close that it startled me a bit. At the set of the hook, it fought hard, trying to snag my line. But in a minute or two, it came to my hand, another foot-long brown. Old Dumpy, I decided, was obviously in one of her more generous moods.

And on a fallen tree that laid across the stream, I paused for a break. There I rested on its trunk in the middle of the creek, Old Dump's current curling and gurgling about my legs… soaking in the beauty and the glory that only a living, breathing trout stream can offer.

No king has ever sat on a more fitting throne, I decided!

I finished my half-mile wade along Old Dump the other afternoon. And I came away leg-sore, bug-bitten, and muck-smudged.

And that's the way it was supposed to be. I'd paid my dues for the nine trout that rested in my creel.

… Dues that Old Dumpy demands from folks like me that come to visit.

June, 1997

Fat-Lipped Muskie

There's a muskie with a fat lip swimming around in a remote northwoods lake these days. It's fat-lipped because a bucktail bait is hanging from its jaw.

The fish, I'm sure, is mean and it's ornery. Yet, it should consider itself lucky. It could well be a statistic, you see, an entry on the chart of big fish that Joe Weiss keeps in his cabin on the lake. Fish that he and his partners have caught.

I'd called Joe, one of the calls that we routinely make to each other to check on who can go fishing.

"Hey!" he said, "I'm just ready to head up to the cabin for a couple days. Come on up!"

Well, I didn't really have two days of fishing in mind at the moment.

"Let me check my agenda," I answered. "I may just take you up on that offer."

And after some heavy juggling of my "excessively-heavy workload." I threw the toothbrush and fishing rods into the pickup, and headed for the back country of Sawyer County.

Weiss greeting me as I pulled in. He was in a sweat... literally. He'd just finished cutting the grass. And the day was hot and steamy.

"Make yourself at home," he said, as he led me into the log structure, cool in the shade of the tall birches and pines

"Joe Weiss is a die-hard muskie fisherman"

"Minnows and Shotgun Shells"

that screen it from both the road and the water.

The place reeks of fishing. All the way from the "Gone Fishing" sign that hangs in the hall to the stuffed muskie over the kitchen door.

"That's my grandfather's old muskie rod," he said, pointing to a well-worn pole hanging on the living room wall. "That's the old Pflueger Supreme reel he used. And that's his old trout fishing creel."

And more.

I wasn't surprised. For to know Joe Weiss is to know fishing. They don't come more hard-nosed in the sport than he is.

Down at the dock, two boats were tied. And after a lunch break, we climbed into the biggest, his musky boat, and headed out. The weather wouldn't be the best, sunny and calm. We'd both suffer in the heat and humidity.

We'd fish the rocky bars and submerged weed beds. I'd work on the walleyes, tossing jigs tipped with leeches.

Joe would test the muskies, casting bucktails and jerk baits, positioning the boat with his electric trolling motor.

And another side of the guy's love for fishing. He makes his own bucktails, baits that he markets around the area under the "MONSTER" lure label. Not often can it be said, that a bait is manufactured and field-tested by the man who fishes with the product himself.

I suppose it was an hour before the first fish action… my good fortune. I felt the tap as the walleye picked up my jig, tightened the line, and set the hook. And shortly, the chunky three-pounder was in the boat.

A half-hour later, a second walleye. Smaller, but a keeper. "Well," I said to Weiss, "I can say that I caught my limit! We'll have those two for supper."

And we did, delicious with au gratin potatoes and a can of

Fat-Lipped Muskie

sweet corn!

I don't know about Weiss, but I slept well that night! Try the recipe... lots of fresh air, some exercise, a hefty fish-fry supper, and a cabin in the northwoods where the only sound is your own snoring!

The next morning found us back on the water. We'd try the same approach, Joe throwing bucktails for muskies, I pitching jigs for walleyes.

And from the top of a shallow weedy bar the muskie came... like out of nowhere.

I was busy tieing on a new jig, just happening to be looking forward toward the bow of the boat where Joe was heaving one of his baits, when the muskie hit.

The water exploded! Right alongside the boat! Right in Weiss' face! And three feet of line hung limply from the tip of his rod!

"He hit just as I was lifting my bait out of the water!" Joe exclaimed, a look of surprise and half-shock on his face.

And the muskie? It disappeared as fast as it appeared. Back to its haunts amidst the mud and the rocks and the weeds. Back to the territory that it claims as its own.

Except for one thing... a bait that dangled from its lip. And it was mad!

And so was the fisherman.

I have a feeling they'll meet again.

June, 1999

The Lady Lifts The Spirit

Things were getting mighty serious around our place last week. What with a trip down south and a bout with bronchitis, I hadn't been fishing for three weeks. That's a long time for me to be out of the fishing loop.

Something had to be done. And I did it. I threw the trout fishing gear into the back of the pickup and headed out.

I'd pay a visit to my old friend, The Beautiful Lady, my favorite stream. The Lady and I have been carrying on together for more than 30 years now. We've shared a lot of good times.

Actually, perhaps I could have waited a day or two. The weather forecast called for thunderstorms and rain. And maybe then I'd catch the Lady when she'd be bankful of water. That's when she's at her best. When there's power in her current. When her rapids echo to her music.

I've been with her, you see, at such times. And it's then that her big brown trout come out to play. When they lose all fear, gobbling fat nightcrawlers that come drifting past their noses without hesitation.

But I couldn't wait. I'd had it with airports, three-lane traffic and strange beds. I needed a fishing fix… and bad. So what if the afternoon was so bright and so sunny that the big browns would be wearing sunglasses! So what if the Lady's

The Lady Lifts The Spirit

water would be so low and clear that every pebble on her bottom would show!

I'd pay her a visit, one that was long overdue. One that would first be a social call, a chance to share her beauty and solitude. The fish? They'd be secondary. Many's been the time that I've waded the Lady not really caring if I caught anything. Just being with her was all that was important.

That's the way it would be this day.

The path I've walked so many times to the stream showed some sign of foot traffic. I'm not the only fisherman that comes the Lady's way. But the spider webs across the trail told me no one had passed of late.

Through the forest the trail wove, the aspens and oaks and pines resplendent now in the lush green of the growing season. A forest has beauty every season of the year. But never so soft and so subtle as now, in late spring, when the plant world is at its peak of renewal.

And finally, through the foliage, a glimpse of the Lady herself... flowing gently, peacefully.

She was in her summer garb, that was obvious, her banks already standing thick with tall marsh grass. I'd missed her at her finest... early May, when the first blush of faint green cloaks her popples, and trilliums stand white amidst her yellow marsh marigolds.

That's when she shines, jewel-like.

And I began my fishing.

Two of my long-favored holes and, except for a few tiny brooks and browns, nothing. And the words of a friend began to cross my mind. The stream wasn't producing this year, he'd told me. Something hard for me to believe, judging by my many years of associating with the Lady.

Upstream I moved, slowly, taking my time. And from a

"Minnows and Shotgun Shells"

rocky run, a keeper brown. No bragger, but then not many of the Lady's trout are.

Ahead, the stream meandered its way through a stretch of swampy bottom, tough going, where a false step in my waders would mean a dunking in cold water. And the casting would be tricky, under low-hanging branches of alder, and across marsh grass draping over the water.

But there'd be more shade. Maybe, with the bright sunshine, there the fish would be. And not 50 feet into the mess, the theory proved true, as I landed a brilliantly-colored foot-long brook trout. And soon, from a deep, shaded bend, a fine brown and another good brookie.

Wading that particular stretch of the Lady always gives me the feeling that I'm on some strange tropical jungle stream. Standing in the hip-deep water with the thick foliage extending high above my head, there's a sensation of being in a kind of secluded "other" world, a personal world rarely known to others.

Yes, I came away from the Beautiful Lady with a fair catch of trout the other day.

But I also came away with something much more important.

… a lighter load on my shoulders!

June, 1998

Summer –

... *The still evening air cools as I fish on; picking up a trout here, another there. On past the truck to the one last hallowed hole.*

Silently I slip around the clump of alders, and almost face-to-face a drinking red-coated deer explodes from the stream, sending water flying, whistling and snorting as it plunges out of sight into the gathering darkness.

The sun has long disappeared, and the first stars blink above me. Off in the woods a young coyote yips a greeting to the night. Tall pine trees stand silhouetted black against the lingering glow of the sunset.

A hot summer night has passed on a trout stream ...

Floating The Namekagon

"Big one on the right!" I called.
"You did a good job of missing that one!" I yelled.
I was back-seat driving so to speak... from the back seat of a fourteen-foot, flat-bottomed Jon boat. And I was shouting instructions to Scottie Hergert, our leader, who was sitting in the middle seat manning the oars.

My shouts were warnings of big rocks lying ahead, just under the surface of the Namekagon River. Rocks that protruded precariously upward from the river's bottom. Boulders that were etched with swatches of silver, evidence left there by aluminum canoes that had bounced off their rugged granite faces.

Three of us were on a float trip down the Namekagon. The idea was Hergert's, who lives in Trego, almost next door to the river. And he'd invited me and Stan Stone, a retired police chief from Illinois, now a permanent resident of our north country, to join him.

Normally, canoes are used to run the river. But the three of us are fishermen, and we wanted to fish as well as float. Thus, Hergert had opted for a flat-bottomed boat. We'd ride the river a bit more leisurely, anchor over some of the deeper holes, and perhaps catch a fish or two.

The plan sounded good to me. While I was familiar with

"Stan Stone (left) and Scottie Hergert float the wild Namekagon River"

"Minnows and Shotgun Shells"

the canoeing qualities and the spectacular scenery of the river, having run it before, I'd never fished it.

And my fishing appetite was whetted more as we visited with Dave Jacoby. Jacoby is one of the owners of Namekagon Outfitters, a canoe rental and shuttle service on the river just west of Trego. Dave would pick us up later in the day downstream at the Whispering Pines landing.

"You'll float about 9 1/2 miles of river," Dave said. "It'll take you five to six hours. The small mouth bass fishing is picking up, and we've had canoeists catch a six-pound walleye and a forty-inch muskie recently."

The river looked ideal as we dropped our boat in. Recent rains had brought the water level to bank-full. A pull or two on the oars by Scottie, and the current grabbed us.

A free-flowing river is a wondrous thing to me. Once on the water, one lets the river take charge. And therein lies its majesty, its constantly changing personality. Riding a fast-moving river is sort of like dancing with a partner who insists on leading. Follow along and things go smoothly. But make a misstep and things go awry. Like hanging up on a rock or tangling with a treetop dangling low over the water.

But that's all part of the fun and challenge. The Namekagon's a relatively placid stream. Not at all like the Upper Flambeau that I told Hergert and Stone about. Where a group of us, experienced canoeists, once put seven canoes in below the Turtle Dam and dumped five of them in the first rapids!

The Namekagon today is part of the National Park Service's wild rivers system. And the reasons are apparent. The river and its shoreline are virtually unspoiled. Entering that environ is like entering another world.

Fish? Well, we tried, throwing all kinds of lures. But only

Floating The Namekagon

Stone had success, a small mouth bass landed and another hooked and lost.

But the scenery! The river twists and turns its way through a valley of steep-sided banks forested with ash, oak, aspen and jack pine. Then, standing periodically at the water's edge are tall, thick-boled, sentinel-like white and Norway pines, relics of the virgin forests that once cloaked the land.

And the wildlife! Like the mother doe that stood drinking with her twin fawns as we approached. Bald eagles that flushed almost in our faces. Overhead, as we passed, cedar waxwings, darted into the air to capture insects we disturbed. Turtles plopped into the water from old logs, and dragonflies flitted, chasing mosquitoes.

Over it all hung the stillness, the solitude, broken only by our voices, the songs of birds, and the beautiful music of the river itself as it gurgled and churned its way.

Then add in a lunch that never tasted better! Dakota bread, fresh from Phil Markgren's bakery, laced with roast pork and fresh lettuce, served by Hergert as we floated gently along, letting the Namekagon take us where it would.

... One can feel rich indeed on the Namekagon.

July, 1994

Big Al, My Boat Buddy

Big Al, my boat, has been neglected of late. For a month, my faithful friend hadn't been in the water, standing instead lonely and forlorn in the garage, twiddling his transom, patiently waiting, while I'd been off giving haircuts to the Christmas trees out at the Tree Farm.

The guilt of it all had been bearing down on me. First things first, your turn will come, I'd rationalized as I'd walked past the big guy each day.

That moment finally arrived the other day.

As I snapped my buddy onto the hitch of the pickup, my conscience began to clear. We'd spend a day together on a little lake somewhere, just the two of us, like things were supposed to be.

Actually, though Big Al was rarin' to go, I wasn't. I was still healing up from long days of swinging a tree-shearing knife. What I had in mind was a quiet, restful fishing trip... one where I could sit on a nice soft boat seat, take it easy, and not work too hard at trying to catch a fish.

An afternoon of bluegill fishing, I decided, would serve us both well. Al would get some exercise. But I wouldn't. I'd just sit back, soak up some sunshine, and rest my weary bones.

At the boat landing, I dropped His Honor into the water,

climbed aboard, and shoved off. And a bit of a testy temperament!

The guy's motor wouldn't start, revenge I'm sure, for the neglect I'd shown. But a loose battery connection was quickly located, and up the lake we purred.

I fish for bluegills a couple of times each summer. It's a nice interlude from the more arduous trout and walleye fishing I do. And it takes me back to my boyhood. Bluegills are usually the first fish that kids catch.

A year ago I'd gone to the lake, and I'd found the gills in the deep water. And as I moved up the lake the other day, I passed over that water, watching the fish locator as I did. To my surprise, I marked very few fish.

And instinct told me to try the shallows first. With Big Al purring happily, I eased up to a weedy flat and dropped the anchor. Rigging a small bobber on the light line of a spinning rod, I set the nightcrawler-baited hook just deep enough to drift before the wind over the top of the weeds.

Call it luck, call it fate! Whatever! But I couldn't have chosen a better spot. Immediately, I was into bluegills. And nice fish in the eight-to-nine-inch range. Fish that were resplendent in their blue-black backs and orange bellies.

And fighters! How they did scrap! No horsing those beauties!

Ah, but this was just what I needed, some relaxing, restful fishing. Nearby a turtle stuck his head out of the water. In the air, dragonflies flitted. Mallards and wood ducks sped past.

And a special touch of excitement as I reeled in my line to make a cast.

Across the water, the little bobber skipped, the worm-baited hook following in its wake. Without warning, the water

"Minnows and Shotgun Shells"

exploded as a good-sized northern pike became airborne, for a full-length landing, like a cat pouncing on a mouse, on my line.

At first I thought it had struck at the bobber, but as my line tightened, I realized the fish was on. Surely it'll break my four-pound line, I thought. But I played it gently, and soon it was in the landing net, a nice 26-incher, close to five pounds.

Mixed with the bluegills, was an occasional crappie that had a taste for worms. Crappies normally prefer minnows.

The fish action slowed as the afternoon wore on, especially when the wind shifted around to the east. Old fishermen have always known that fish bite least when the wind's in the east.

Quitting time came, and Al and I headed for the landing. In the live well, splashed the half-limit of bluegills that I'd set for myself, makins' for some mighty fine fish suppers.

Big Al, my old pal, and I had enjoyed a good day together.

August, 1997

Summer Trout Miseries

A person has to be some kind of a sadist, one who enjoys pain and suffering, to fish for trout this time of the year. At least on the little cricks that I like to fish. That's what I decided the other day, as I limped my way slowly back to my truck.

Trout fishing has always had its bad sides. Especially in the dead of summer. Like now. But this summer is the pits.

Like when I fished two of my long-time favorite streams recently, Old Dumpy and The Beautiful Lady. I know them well. I've waded their bottoms for a good thirty years!

So how did I do? Well, here's the score, as best I can figure... 2,486 mosquitoes, 1,671 deer flies, two tons of tromped-down marsh grass, and eight measly trout!

And that doesn't count the strained back muscles that I got from crawling over two newly-built beaver dams! Or my itching hands from a couple of brushings against stinging nettles. Or several gallons of sweat from the heat and the humidity.

Oh... one more thing. The other day I thought sure I was going to need an ear transplant, the bugs were chewing on it so bad... as I stood in the crick trying to tie on a new hook.

I'm beginning to think I've only got one oar in the water when it comes to trout fishing this time of year!

"Minnows and Shotgun Shells"

So why do I go? Well, my motivation springs from all the rain we've been getting. I like to fish when the water's high. That's when, I've found, that the fish bite the best. And that's when the streams are the most fun. The water's deep, the current's strong, and the rapids sing their loudest music.

But sometimes you can have too much of a good thing. This summer we've had a lot of rain. True, the streams have been bankful. But so have the marshes and swamps which drain into the streams.

Add in the hot, sunny days we've been receiving, and there the water sits, gathering heat. By the time it reaches the stream, it's lukewarm.

The result, as I see it, is a superabundance of streamside vegetation, marsh grass so thick that in many places the stream is completely hidden.

It's great for the trout. There they relax in the shade of the grassy canopy, living high on the hog on insects and minnows that the warmer-than-usual water produces.

And the poor fishermen, like me, can't even get at the fish! Try casting a nightcrawler into a small pocket of water through a curtain of tall marsh grass waving in the breeze! The narrow deeper sections of the streams become virtually unfishable. And that's where the smart trout hang out.

And the vegetation growth within the streams themselves is also heavy. Which too cuts down on the amount of fishable water.

So I go to what my old Park Falls friend, Ed Sealander, a good trout fisherman himself, used to call "dabbling." Dabbling is fishing with a very short line, maybe only six feet, to drop a bait in small pockets of open water along the banks. It's fun to see a trout suddenly dart out to grab the bait.

Sure, there are a few spots where the fisherman can still

Summer Trout Miseries

get a line into the water decently. Places like deep pools and bends where the current keeps the bottom scoured. And if you know the crick well and sneak up on those holes, you stand a fair chance of catching a fish.

Like the last spot I fished the other day.

A big willow tree had blown down across the crick since I was there the last time, and the trunk had caused the current to scour out a nice new hole.

"Hmmm!" I said to myself, "I have to give this a try!" And I flipped my nightcrawler upstream alongside the tree trunk. Only I didn't see a branch sticking out, which snagged my line.

Well, I didn't want to disturb the hole, so I broke the line and proceeded to tie on a new hook. (That's when I thought I'd need my ear transplant.)

Well, my second cast went where I wanted it to, and immediately a trout nailed it. I landed the fish, a dandy brook trout... and when I lifted it from the water, there hanging from its mouth was my lost hook and a piece of line. The broken line must have fallen into the water, and the trout had grabbed it!

A fitting close to a day that proved two things.

One, that the trout was dumb.

And two, that the old itching, stinging, scratching, swatting, sweating, sore-muscled, mud-stained fisherman who caught it isn't too swift either.

August, 1999

Alaska Fishing Guide

"Sometimes I'd be beat... but every day, I'd say to myself, this is a paid vacation!"

So Pete Mommsen, of Spooner, describes his past summer's job, that of a fishing guide in Alaska.

A third-year college student, majoring in education at the University of Wisconsin-Stout, Mommsen comes from a guiding family. Both his father and grandfather have served as guides here in Wisconsin.

"I'd guided a little around here," Pete told. "I wanted the experience (Alaska), and my dad pushed me to go."

Mommsen found his summer employment via the Internet. "I sent out about 50 resumés," he explained. "I got responses from about half of them. It got down to three choices, and I picked a lodge at King Salmon."

King Salmon is a community of 1500 located about 300 miles southwest of Anchorage, accessible only by float plane and boat.

"I picked the place because of the money, and because it's on the coast," he said. "The closer to the ocean, the better the salmon fishing. He was one of four guides provided by the 48-room lodge. Guests come both to fish and to watch the many Alaska brown bears in the area.

"I was on the Naknek River," Mommsen said. "It's a

good-sized river, and we used 20-foot boats with 150 horsepower motors. My clients came from the Midwest, California and Georgia. They were very serious fishermen. Lots of professional people! They spend thousands of dollars to come and fish."

Species caught included king, silver, pink and chumm salmon, rainbow trout, grayling and northern pike. The salmon run up Alaska's rivers from the ocean in the summer to spawn.

"Before the kings started running in June, we fished for rainbows," he continued. "It was nothing to catch 24 to 30-inch fish."

The king salmon, however, were the most popular. "It's like fighting a 35 pound musky that won't quit!" he said. "The king just won't play out! Sometimes we caught 10 to 15 a day, fish between 25 and 50 pounds! We used heavy tackle with 20-pound line and trolled with spinners and plugs."

Fly fishing was popular for the smaller salmon and rainbows. "Fly fishing is the way to go," Mommsen said.

Clients also enjoyed bear watching. Fly-in trips into the Katmai National Park to the Brooks River Visitor Center were available. "There people can see 50 to 75 bears at one time," Mommsen said. "They (Park Service) have viewing platforms where you can watch the bears safely."

Bears were also common along the fishing streams. "You could see 5 to 15 a day," Mommsen said. "I've had them within 15 feet of me. They seem like they want to check you out; and you stand up, wave your arms, and try to look big. I always carried a 12 gauge loaded with buckshot. But I never had to fire a shot. If you saw one with cubs, you tried to get out of the way as quick as possible!"

In August, Mommsen received an offer to work at a sec-

"Minnows and Shotgun Shells"

ond lodge, which was located more inland. "It was totally different," he said. "More remote, no town, no boats. All the fishing was done by wading and all by fly fishing.

"It was more rustic. They had little cabins for the employees. You couldn't sleep in tents because of the bears.

"It was nice to see both kinds of places in my summer. Coastal Alaska is totally different from the interior. On the coast, you plan your fishing around the tides."

His summer's work left a strong impression on Mommsen. "Between the two places, it was such a diverse summer," he said. "I got to see so much of Alaska. I saw lots of moose, caribou, seals, whales and foxes. All the while, Mount McKinley was present in our fishing. Everywhere you go, it's just gorgeous!"

Mommsen plans to complete his college education, then possibly go back to Alaska to teach. "I'll probably go back next summer to guide again," he said. "I've got so many connections now!"

"Everybody up there is there because they love it," he commented. "There's a totally different attitude, and it wears off on you."

Pete Mommsen's work weeks were never less than 80 hours, he said, what with the long hours of daylight.

Hard, tiring work that at times left him exhausted.

Yet... a most rewarding dream-come-true experience.

September, 1999

Ed Robinson... River Guide

A remote boat landing on the Flambeau River near Butternut got a new name the other day. Known in the past as merely a public landing, like most of its kind around the state, it's now called "Robinson Landing."

It's named for Ed Robinson, a man who's legendary as a guide on the river. But more than that, he's a man who loves the river like no other... a man who's been a powerful influence on the river's character, as we know it today.

And therein lies another side of the story that was told the other morning, as the Wisconsin DNR erected a handsome sign that now bears Robinson's name... a sign that assures that he'll be remembered for generations to come for his contributions toward preserving probably the finest stretch of big-river water left in the state.

The river's side of the story begins back in the early 1980's when a large corporation, owner of lands adjacent to both sides of the Flambeau, offered to sell some 13 miles of frontage to the state. The land in question, a strip 300 feet wide, represented some of the finest natural fauna left in northern Wisconsin, pristine with pine, hemlock and other northern forest tree species.

The river itself was spectacular, free-flowing in a near-primitive condition, replete with rock ledges and white-

"Ed Robinson guided fishermen on river trips for 68 years. Following his death in 1998, he was inducted into the Freshwater Fishing Hall of Fame at Hayward, Wisconsin"

water rapids. And talks began with local citizens, town boards, and county boards on the merits of acquiring the lands being offered. The establishment of a natural area to forever preserve the unique character of the river was proposed.

And from those discussions came Ed Robinson's point of view, his concerns.

Over the many years that he'd guided on the river, he'd come to know it well, perhaps better than any other human. He too wanted the river left as it had been created. And when management policy was formulated for the proposed natural area, Ed Robinson's thinking was a major force on the shaping of that policy.

For example, one of the features of the management planning was the creation of an advisory committee comprised of local citizens. Its purpose would be to assure that communication would continue between DNR personnel and local people, that they'd have a voice in decisions that would affect the river.

And in 1985, when the land purchase was culminated and the natural area established, Ed Robinson was named to that citizens advisory committee, a post that he has held to this day.

"His counsel has been instrumental in guiding the department (DNR) on the management of this property," Dave Olson, superintendent of the Flambeau River State Forest, said the other day as he presented a plaque of appreciation to Robinson.

I knew Ed Robinson back in those early 1980 times, and I was pleased to be present at the ceremony last week that honored him. Now 83 years old, he's still busy guiding people down his beloved Flambeau, riding its waters in his

"Minnows and Shotgun Shells"

wooden flat-bottomed riverboat.

"It's been a great life," he told me. "I've been a guide for 68 years, the last 58 here on the Flambeau. I've guided people from all over the world. I've made at least 5,000 trips down the river and have guided at least 10,000 people!"

Two now-retired DNR officials spoke of Ed Robinson's help.

"Ed's been a supporter of this project and always will be," said Cully Erickson, former superintendent of the Flambeau River State Forest.

"A lot of words of wisdom came out of Ed Robinson," said Paul Gottwald, retired area supervisor. "That's HIS river!"

And what better words than those from Robinson himself!

Standing there amongst his friends and admirers, wearing his red floppy felt guide's hat and knee-high rubber boots, he said it all.

"I want this river to stay as it is," he told me. "I'd like to see my grandkids go down the river and see it as it is today."

I came away from that very nice ceremony the other day with a final thought.

There's a fine line, I decided, between the Flambeau River and Ed Robinson. I say that because the river is so much a part of Ed Robinson.

… And then, Ed Robinson is so much a part of the river.

July, 1997

An Otter Kind of Fishing

Strange things happen on trout streams I've found. Like the times I trip and fill my waders with cold water. Or a colorful character I meet. Perhaps some interesting wildlife that I bump into.

Like the other day when... well, let me tell you about it.

Folks occasionally ask me what my favorite kind of fishing is. The question's not easy to answer. I like many kinds of fishing. And I pause each time to meditate a bit before answering.

Trout fishing always comes out on top. Trout fishing's a lot like taking a hike through the woods, except the trail is a streambed. Trout fishing puts a person in close contact with nature... birds, animals, snakes, turtles. And vegetation like trees and wildflowers.

Add in the fact, as I believe, that trout fishing is a solitary sport, best done alone. Trout fishing allows one to enjoy the finest of nature's solitude and beauty. I've said many times that I can lose the world on a mile of trout stream.

Such were my thoughts the other day as I slipped on my waders, gathered my gear, and headed along a trail toward one of the streams I fish. Behind me, finished, were the summer work projects that had occupied much of my time. I was ready for a day off, a day of celebration... on a trout stream.

"Minnows and Shotgun Shells"

Carefully, I picked my way through the waist-high marsh grass, watchful of the nettles that sting and burn the skin. Into the stream I waded to begin my casting. The first pool, a good one that usually produces a nice fish, yielded nothing. And upstream I moved, picking my way over deadfalls and sandbars.

The stream was in excellent shape. Apparently the thunderstorms of the day before had dumped some rain on its headwaters. A good flow was coming down. And the first trout, a small brookie, from an undercut bank draped with marsh grass. Lightly hooked, I returned it to the water. And a second, one for the creel, from a deep hole where the current cuts hard as it rounds a bend.

Casually, I worked my way, studying the stream, enjoying every foot of it. Three hours, a half-mile, and as I approached my favorite stretch of water, the creel held nine trout, one shy of the limit.

To the toe of the run I'd sneaked, quietly, stealthily, to place my casts as perfectly as possible. And then something strange! Upstream I noticed some unusual undulations in the water, like something swimming below the surface. Probably a beaver, I thought. I've had them swim almost between my legs.

CRASH! Suddenly, only a few yards in front of me, the water exploded, like a big muskie hitting a surface plug. And out of the water came the head of a big otter with a dandy brook trout in its mouth. I say "dandy" because the otter's head was close to six inches across, yet there was trout sticking out both sides of its mouth!

Though completely startled, I didn't move. Across the stream, the otter swam in full view, into the marsh grass to thrash and splash as it fed on the trout. Finished, back it

An Otter Kind of Fishing

came, swimming, its sleek head and neck extending above the water.

Then, from behind a clump of alders, a second otter appeared. And a splash in the shallows to my right told me of a third. Suddenly I was almost surrounded by swimming otters! I'd seen quite a few over time, but none ever as close as this.

Of course, they soon spotted me. Out of the water, two rose to look me over. There we were, almost eyeball to eyeball, as they called to each other with a grunt-like 'hah... hah... hah' sound of alarm. Then, with a whirl and a splash, they were gone, retreating upstream from whence they'd come.

Like I say, strange things happen on trout streams. My close encounter with the three otters will stick in my mind forever.

And did they catch all the trout? No, I finished out my limit with a dandy foot-long brookie.

Just like the one in my otter friend's mouth.

August, 1994

Hang A Right In Sidnaw

Two places in Michigan's Upper Peninsula hold special meaning for me. One is a little town, the other is a wilderness lake.

Last week's column delved at considerable length into the four days I spent recently in the U.P. with two fishing friends, Johnny Walker and Dick Birkholz. My words spoke to the trip, the wildlife we saw, the rustic cabin we occupied, and the fishing we experienced on Lake Gogebic and the Bond Flowage.

The story, however, deliberately by-passed my two favorite places, the little town and the wilderness lake.

First the town.

It's called Sidnaw. Run your fingers easterly along Highway 28 across a map of the U.P., past places like Berglund, Bruce Crossing and Trout Creek, and you'll come to Sidnaw. It's kind of out in the middle of nowhere.

I've been to Sidnaw in years past. Walker, Burkholz and I have passed its way, sometimes pausing, as we did the other day, for breakfasts at the Sunshine Cafe, Sidnaw's one and only eating place.

From our table by the front window, I looked the town over once again. Across the street, a tall spruce tree rustled in the breeze. Along the curb, white and lavender petunias

"Upper Michigan's Perch Lake yielded a walleye to Johnny Walker"

"Minnows and Shotgun Shells"

bloomed, planted as a civic project in half-whiskey-barrel pots. And along the sidewalk strolled a nattily-dressed lady senior citizen, typical of the retired folks who make up most of the hundred or so town's citizens.

Some might say that time has passed Sidnaw by. I say no. I say time hasn't yet caught up to Sidnaw. For Sidnaw comes across to me as a place of supreme peace... something we could use a lot more of in this world.

Sidnaw's more, however. Sidnaw's a jumping-off place for Walker, Birkholz and me. It's there that we turn off to travel to Perch Lake, my second special-meaning place.

Twelve miles, we travel through the back country, the road gradually changing from blacktop to gravel and finally to sandy dirt. Along its twisting, turning way, one can still recognize, if one has an eye for such things, the history of the area. Old clearings, sagging barb-wire fences, and scraggly apple trees tell of pioneer settlers. Aspen and jack pine forests grow where fierce forest fires once burned.

And at the end of the trail lies Perch Lake, a jewel of wild water surrounded by the forest primeval of the Ottawa National Forest. On its shores stand hemlocks and maples three feet through on the stump, remnants of the virgin forest that once cloaked the land.

Perch is a good fishing lake. Walker, Birkholz and I have been there several times, both summer and winter. We come to do battle with its walleyes.

Thus we did that recent day.

Out of the northeast, off Lake Superior, a cool breeze blew, tempering the heat of the bright sun shining from a cloudless blue sky. Perch is about a thousand acres in size, I'd estimate, shallow and weedy.

Our fishing strategy was simple. Drift slowly downwind

over the weeds and cast jigs tipped with minnows or rubber imitation minnows. Wherever we fished, we caught walleyes. One bay, so weedy that years back I named it Walker's Swamp, was particularly productive.

There, though every other cast resulted in a gob of green on our hooks, we caught fish on every drift. And also along the edges of the bull-rush beds that line the shore in places.

Sounds good, you say? Well, it was. There was a downside, however. Michigan has a 15-inch minimum size limit on walleyes, and of the 50 or so we caught, only three were large enough to keep.

And we weren't alone. Two other fishermen who came into the landing as we were loading our boat told of the same kind of luck.

But fishing is a lot more than putting fish on a stringer. Fishing's an outdoor experience. And that's what my day had been... a visit back to the beautiful lake, good companions, a shore lunch beneath towering trees, and an immense solitude.

All part of fishing in the forest primeval.

Hang a hard right in downtown Sidnaw... that's how it's found.

September, 1997

Big Al's A Sly Rat

Big Al, my boat pal, finally got a chance to go fishing the other day. The old boy gets a little puckered this time of the year... when I don't give him what he considers to be his proper due.

There he rests in the garage, impatiently twiddling his transom, while I'm off shearing Christmas trees, or as this summer, gallivanting around to a family reunion. And the big guy tries to get some revenge... letting his batteries run down, maybe softening one of his trailer tires... little things intended to irritate me.

I'm used to it. It happens every year.

So the other day, after I'd called Bob Dreis to see if he'd like to join me for some bluegill fishing, I gave Al a good going-over... some time with the battery charger on both his cranking and trolling motor batteries. And I treated him to some fresh gas in his tank. From stem to stern, I checked him out, pampering him, hoping to get back into his good graces.

And off we went, Dreis and I, to my favorite bluegill lake with Al in tow.

Everything looked fine. The little boat landing was deserted, plenty of room to turn around and to park. And with confidence in my heart, I dumped the big guy into the water.

"Climb aboard! We're off to slay the bluegills!" I opti-

"Bob Dreis and a fine crappie"

"Minnows and Shotgun Shells"

mistically announced to Dreis, as we pushed off.

Well, I should have known better. I should have known that Al, sly rat that he is, would have one last trick up his sleeve! Last year it was a loose connection on his battery. This time, it was a balky switch, the one that hydraulically raises and lowers the motor. Up yes! Down, no!

And as Al floated before a brisk wind that was pushing us into some swampy water weeds, I have to admit that I thought some rather unkind things about the guy.

Anyway, his little temper tantrum didn't last. I fiddled with his switch, and in short order, things were back to normal. A couple of spins of his motor, a bit of choking, and Big Al was himself, purring with pride.

Up the lake, Dreis and I motored to a shallow, weedy mud flat. There a year ago I'd found the bluegills thick as fleas, hungry as cornfield-raiding raccoons.

Our fishing technique would be simple. A small hook, a small sinker, a small bobber, and a small piece of nightcrawler for bait. Cast the rig out, let the wind drift it slowly over the weeds, and wait for the bobber to bob.

And while waiting, just settle back on a nice soft comfortable boat seat and enjoy the day.

That would be the best part. To just relax. Like I recall fishing trips as a boy. No frantic cast, cast, cast! There's no ego-tripping in bluegill fishing, no worrying about a trophy for the wall. Just plain old-fashioned simple angling, with the bonus of taking a meal or two home for the table.

And that's the way things worked out. The fish, the bluegills and an occasional crappie, cooperated. Not as aggressively as a year ago. Just steady. Every few minutes either Bob or I would have one on, our line slicing sideways through the water as the good-sized fish scrapped.

And what a day to be out on a northern Wisconsin lake! For most of it, Dreis and I were the only fishermen... the peace, the beauty and the solitude hanging over the water, for us alone to enjoy.

Overhead, hung a summer sky of blue dappled with white cottony clouds, tempering the coolness of the brisk northwest breeze, fresh in from Canada.

Riding the wind was a bald eagle, wings outstretched as it soared, majestic in its black body and snow-white head and tail. A red-tailed hawk circled high overhead, and tree swallows swooped over the water's surface, feeding on insects.

By early afternoon, as other fishermen began to arrive, Big Al's livewell splashed with a decent catch of panfish, fish that are aptly named. Because that was where they were headed... as fillets in a frying pan at an upcoming supper with friends.

Dreis and I had had a good day. And Big Al too, apparently.

The Big Guy ran perfectly... no more of his dirty tricks to torment me!

August, 1998

Aspen Is Important

On a fishing trip to northern Minnesota recently, my partner, Bruce Moss, and I got into a conversation about the prospects for our upcoming ruffed grouse hunting season. Moss is a veteran DNR wildlife biologist stationed at Spooner.

Moss said that this year's spring drumming counts, a survey to index the grouse population, looked quite promising, that the bird's numbers appear to be on the increase. Which is good news for those of us who enjoy crisp October afternoons afield with our shotguns... our faithful, hard-working hunting dogs at our side.

When it comes to quality recreation, there is no finer sport that ruffed grouse hunting, I say. I've done my share, enjoying those days immensely.

Yet, on the horizon looms some news that's not good, news that those of us who cherish our grouse should heed.

The down-side news came from two directions. First, in the spring newsletter, "The Drumming Log", put out by the Ruffed Grouse Society, a national organization of grouse lovers. And second, in a report I received at a forestry meeting at Hayward. Titled "Wisconsin Forest Statistics, 1996," the report documents data recovered from the recently-conducted fifth inventory of Wisconsin's forests. Inventories

Aspen Is Important

have been conducted at about 15-year intervals, starting in the 1930's.

And how do these two documents tie in with our grouse hunting?

The answer to that question lies in one word... "aspen".

Aspen is a relatively short-lived species of tree. Often called "popple", it's found commonly throughout our north. It's a tree that's valuable for many reasons. Economically, aspen is used for a wide variety of wood products. Aspen logs are manufactured in large quantities into paper, chipboard and lumber. Trucks travel our highways daily, carrying logs that represent jobs and paychecks for land owners, woods workers, and mill employees alike.

Aspen adds to our scenic northwoods beauty. Come fall, its brilliant gold foliage brightens our roadsides. In the summer, a breeze rustling through its trembling leaves brings music to the ear of the trout fisherman.

Last, but not least, is aspen's value to wildlife. Aspen is a sun-loving plant. It grows best in full sunlight. And, as would be expected, it has friends, other associated plants, that also are sun lovers. Together they form an ecological complex of protein-rich nutritious vegetation, habitat that is excellent, the best, for most species of wildlife... especially grouse.

In my recent "Drumming Log," Dan Dessecker, a wildlife biologist for the Ruffed Grouse Society, explains that ruffed grouse populations in the Great Lakes area are inexorably tied to the aspen resource. As aspen goes, so go ruffed grouse.

So what's the problem, you say?

Well, the answer to that question lies in the data from our recent forest inventory.

"Minnows and Shotgun Shells"

Aspen forest acreage is declining in Wisconsin. Here in northwest Wisconsin, the 1996 inventory found 1,385,000 acres of aspen. The 1983 survey found 1,508,000 acres, a decrease of 123,000 acres.

That's a lot of wildlife habitat to be degraded in only 13 years!

And where did that land go? Well, it didn't just disappear. It's still out there, still growing trees. The problem is that it isn't growing aspen trees, and aspen's sun-loving friends, any more.

Why, you ask?

In most cases, the reason lies in less-than-desirable forest management by landowners. Aspen must be clearout. Clearcutting exposes the forest floor to the heat of the sun, causing the roots of the parent stand to sprout into literally thousands of young aspen shoots, thereby assuring an aspen forest for the future.

Clearcutting, or complete removal of the parent stand, tends to be emotional. Yet it's akin to a farmer removing a crop of corn or hay from his field. A clearcut doesn't destroy a forest. Properly done, the reverse is true. The aspen forest is regenerated and preserved for the future. In the process, food and shelter are created for not only ruffed grouse, but most of our other wildlife species as well.

The ecological trend that our aspen forest land is taking should be cause for concern for all of us who value our north as we've known it.

Generations of tomorrow will have to live with what we do, or don't do, today!

July, 1998

Terry Brown Teaches Safety

An important position was filled by the Wisconsin Department of Natural Resources at Spooner recently. Terry Brown, a veteran conservation officer, was named to head the several outdoor safety programs that the department carries out here in northwest Wisconsin.

I say the job is important for two reasons. Number one, over the past 20-some years, I've witnessed the successes that have been achieved. And number two, because as a hunter and fisherman all my life, and having had a few close calls of my own, I appreciate how easily accidents can happen in the outdoors.

Brown's job will be to prevent such accidents from happening. And he'll try to do that by coordinating the teachings of a small army of volunteer instructors... men and women who will educate folks, mostly youngsters, on safe conduct in our woods and on our waters.

Brown comes to the Spooner DNR district office from Barron County, where he's served as a warden since 1988. He, his wife and three children live in Rice Lake.

A 1973 graduate of the University of Wisconsin-Stevens Point with a degree in wildlife management, Brown worked at the DNR fish hatchery at Woodruff and on the Northern Highland State Forest at Trout Lake before becoming a warden.

"Warden Terry Brown heads outdoor safety programs in northwest Wisconsin"

Terry Brown Teaches Safety

The Wisconsin DNR is responsible for the administration of five outdoor safety education programs: gun hunting, bow hunting, boating, snowmobile, and all-terrain-vehicle operation. In each instance, classes are held throughout the state, using education materials produced by people like Brown and his counterparts.

As said, the instruction is provided by volunteers.

"They're very self-motivated, unselfish, community-minded individuals," Brown said. "They love their sports and want to share that with young adults. They donate thousands of hours. My job is to work with them and keep the programs going smoothly."

Brown will also work closely with DNR field wardens who are stationed in the 12 counties under the district programs. Field wardens serve as local coordinators of the safety workshops. They're also responsible for the investigation of accidents that occur.

With our fall hunting seasons upon us, Brown had some advice for those of us going afield.

"Remember the three safety rules," he said. "First, treat every firearm as if it were loaded. Second, be sure of your target and beyond. And third, always control the muzzle of the firearm."

He also urges small-game hunters to wear a piece of blaze orange, a hat or vest. During the gun deer season, 50% of the upper body clothing and hat must be blaze orange.

"Blaze orange and safety instruction are the most important safety items we have," he said. "Hunting accidents from guns have steadily declined, though the number of hunters has steadily increased since the hunter safety education program began in 1967. In 1997, we certified 30,000 kids in the state."

"Minnows and Shotgun Shells"

While safe gun handling is stressed, the course also teaches survival skills, first aid, hunting ethics, and landowner respect.

Brown also had some words of caution for waterfowl hunters and fall fishermen.

"This is a prime time of the year to suffer hypothermia," he warned. "Boaters should wear their life preservers. Hunters should wear camo float coats and float pants. They'll keep you warm and dry."

Brown will also help municipalities that wish to draft and adopt local ordinances dealing with beach safety, slow-wake areas, channel buoy placement, and snowmobile and ATV travel. Communities seeking assistance should contact their local wardens who will then inform Brown of their interest.

He will also work with sheriff departments that have snowmobile and ATV enforcement patrols.

I said at the outset that Terry Brown's job is an important one. Yet the effectiveness of his work is hard to measure. How, for example, does one count the number of accidents that are prevented... the injuries, and yes, even deaths, that do NOT occur because of his work?

Such numbers never show, yet we who use the outdoors know they exist.

That impact on our society was well-reflected in Terry Brown's final words the other day.

"The kids are so much fun to work with!" Brown said. "It's so nice to have a youngster come back and hear him or her say 'you were my hunter safety instructor!'"

September, 1998

Bluegills At Their Best

Some of the best bluegill fishing I've ever had! That's what I'd have to say about a recent outing.

All summer long, I've had a hankerin' for some tasty bluegill fillets. Twice, I'd tried the critters. But without much success.

That changed the other day, however.

One more try, I told myself, I'd give the fish. And I picked a day. But then, out of Canada, rolled a cold front. And with it, a blustery northwest wind.

I watched the backyard trees sway before the breeze, as I sipped a second cup of coffee, mentally debating whether I should postpone the trip. Nothing takes the fun out of a fishing trip faster than fighting a wind in a boat.

Maybe I'd be smart to go trout fishing instead, I meditated. Wind on a trout stream can be an advantage. It keeps the bugs down.

But then, an old fishing partner, Joe Zanter, drove into the yard. Was he interested in going fishing, I asked? Certainly, he answered.

Well, that clinched the decision. We'd try the bluegills. And if they weren't cooperative, we'd give the northern pike and walleyes a look... wind or no wind! The worse that could happen would be that we'd be forced to fish the lee

"Minnows and Shotgun Shells"

side of the lake.

And with that we headed out with Big Al, my boat, in tow. Big Al is living it up these days. I put new wheels under him recently, trading my old bunk-bed trailer for one of those new-fangled roller-bed kind, making Big Al's unloading and loading a lot easier. Which is nice for old codgers like Zanter and me.

As I expected, the lake was kicking up real good as I steered Big Al toward the open water. On both sides of the channel, a thick bed of tall wild rice swayed before the gale.

As fate would have it, the weedy bar that I wanted to fish was located on the east side of the lake, where the water was the roughest. But we'd give it a try anyway.

And I put the boat on a downwind drift toward the bar. We'd cast jigs tipped with minnows for northerns and walleyes in the deeper water until my depth-finder told me we were over the bar.

Which worked fine. We didn't catch any northerns or walleyes, but we did find the bar. I dropped the anchor, and we proceeded to rig our rods for bluegills.

And the gills were there. I caught a couple dandies right away. The trouble was that we couldn't hold the boat… the wind blowing us off the bar as fast as I positioned Big Al.

"Joe, this isn't going to work!" I said to Zanter. "We're going to have to fish the other side, out of the wind." And across the lake, we moved.

Well, I'd never fished that corner of the lake before; and it took a little exploring, but we finally found the bluegills.

The fish were schooled in about 12 feet of water where a thick weed bed fringed out to clean bottom. There in the scattered submerged weeds, the fish were suspended.

Our fishing didn't require much skill. Just hang a line over

Bluegills At Their Best

the side baited with a chunk of nightcrawler and wait for a fat bluegill to bite.

The fish ran nice for size, averaging about eight inches. The biggest I caught measured 9 1/2 inches on the yardstick fastened to the side of the boat. We had several that approached that size. Nice bluegills anywhere!

And it was fun. Every once in awhile, I enjoy just plain taking it easy on a fishing trip. No cast, cast, cast! None of the cold fingers that go with ice fishing! Just settle back on a soft boat seat, soak up some warm sunshine, and fish the way I did when I was a kid.

That's how Zanter and I spent the day. Add in some cheese and crackers and a cold can of pop, and some good natured jibes about our mutual fishing skills, or lack thereof, and a person can come away feeling that he's re-discovered what fishing is supposed to be all about.

Eagles circled the lake above us, and blue-wing teal buzzed the wild rice bed. Except for two other boats that came out briefly, we were the only fishermen on the water!

For a fishing trip born in doubt, it had turned into a good one.

September, 1999

Fall –

... Fall, the glory time! The earth rests after a hard summer's work.

You can feel it in the subtle change in the wind out of the north as it drifts in off Lake Superior. No longer does it have that soft, gentle, cool caress. Now there's a touch of power in it; and a primeval instinct in us stirs, warning that it's time to get moving. The hazy, lazy days of summer are over.

And you can sense it in the deeper azure blue of the sky and the warm, no longer hot, rays of the sun. One side of me basks while my shade side feels good in a wool shirt.

The roadsides and abandoned clearings are splotched with the colors of late summer wildflowers. As if some mad painter has thrown his brushes at the countryside...

Acorns Grow Oaks and Deer

Acorns rattle off our roof these nights. The little marble-like missiles come from a big red oak that towers over the house, over our bedroom.

There I lie, awake with my mid-night insomnia, pondering life in general, and 'plop', an acorn slams on the shingles. 'Pitter-patter,' the noisy nut rolls its way downward, ending its slide with a 'ping' as it drops into the rain gutter.

Some years, when the acorn crop is heavy, the nightly drumming is a steady serenade. Other years, like last, there's silence... signalling that the crop has failed, that Mother Nature couldn't find the right equation the preceding spring to pollinate the flower buds of my oak tree, the conception process from which acorns are born.

I listened to the patter of the acorns the other night, and slowly, gradually my thoughts turned to trees, something I'm very fond of, then to deer and other forms of wildlife, and finally to people, to us, the human race.

Almost imperceptibly, an image began to form in my mind of the importance, the significance, of the tiny green spheres that were dribbling downward. The nuts, I decided, were a vital connection in the world that laid just outside my bedroom window.

There's an old adage that asks a rhetorical question:

Acorns Grow Oaks and Deer

which came first, the chicken or the egg? The same can be said about acorns and oak trees.

Care, I do not. All that matters is that oak trees are a crucial component of the woods that grace our northern Wisconsin landscape. Without acorns, there'd be no oak trees of the future.

So what, I found myself thinking. Certainly mankind is smart enough to exist without oak trees.

Perhaps. But certainly not as well. For oak trees and acorns play a mighty important role in the wildlife populations we value so highly.

Across my desk of late have flowed a number of news stories about the hunting seasons that are now arriving. And in those stories were analyses and projections of the populations of the various game species; deer, bear, ruffed grouse, woodcock, squirrels, and more.

Read those accounts and one quickly learns that much of our wildlife depends on, and benefits from, forest habitat such as oak trees and acorns. Acorns are nutritious, and a bountiful crop means that animals and birds enter the winter, when fat reserves become critical, in good condition. Survival is more probable, and a healthy population more likely the following year.

Deer are a classic example. All summer I've seen deer commonly in my travels, on roadsides, along field edges. Not of late, however. And I'm surmising that I'm not because the critters are hanging back in the cover, feeding on newly-fallen acorns.

And acorns and people?

In our home, as in many, stand pieces of oak furniture; dressers, tables and chairs fashioned from oak lumber, from trees that grew to maturity from tiny acorns. Products all the way from firewood to paper to panelling and flooring are made of oak. Oak lumber is both beautiful and durable.

Ah ha, some will say. At last! A conflict! One of man colliding with his environment, of man desecrating the very resource he professes to value.

Well, yes and no. Such critics are certainly correct when oak forests are indiscriminately slashed for quick profit. But no, if such forests are managed responsibly, with professional forestry help from people who understand the life processes of oak trees.

A great deal of high-quality research has been, and is being, carried out on the science of managing oak forests. All the way from selective thinnings to regeneration techniques. And such research guides the responsible forest manager.

I covered a lot of mental ground the other night as I listened to the rattle and roll of acorns falling on the roof. Those little green nuts, I decided, are certainly a lot more than nuisances, something for me to soon rake up.

They're a critical cog in the complex linkages of the environment around me, I concluded.

… Well worth a couple of hours of lost sleep.

September, 1996

Wild Boars Are Not Boring

Wild boars are definitely not boring! So say three Spooner hunters who have travelled to central Iowa the past two Novembers to pursue the animals.

"Down there, they call them 'poor man's grizzlies'," said Gary Magnus... the implication being that the boars are not only challenging to hunt, but dangerous to be around.

"There's no predicting them," Jeff Mortier added. "You just don't know where they'll be."

"We learned what the words 'full bore', 'boar's nest' and 'hog wild' mean! commented Bill Hoyt.

The three men are avid bow-and-arrow hunters. All spend a great deal of time each fall trying to bag a trophy buck during Wisconsin's archery deer season.

However, that season closes in November the week before the deer gun season. And two years ago, the three began to look for alternative bow-and-arrow hunting opportunities.

"We talked to Butch Bassett, who runs an archery business west of town," one said. "He suggested that we try the wild boar hunting in Iowa."

Bassett further suggested that they try the North Star Gameland Shooting Preserve at Montour, Iowa. The 750-acre preserve provides hunting opportunities for a wide range of wildlife species. In addition to wild boar; deer, elk,

"Hunting wild boars with bow and arrow is exciting sport for (l-r) Gary Magnus, Jeff Mortier and Bill Hoyt"

bison, mountain goats, rams and turkeys are available.

The three were joined by Tom Ennis. "Tom went along to be our cook," Magnus said. "But you can hunt down there with a crossbow, so that's what he used."

All four hunters bagged wild boars that first trip. Mortier's was the largest, a monstrous 404-pound animal.

"Everybody said, why don't you go to a farm and shoot a pig," Mortier noted. "Well, it wasn't like that at all!"

The preserve is very rugged terrain, they found.

"It's all up and down with hills," Hoyt said. "There's oak woods and lots of brush. I must have picked up my hat a thousand times after it was pulled off by thorny locust brush. I've hunted deer since 1950, but I've never worked so hard!"

Their hunting techniques consisted of making drives to one another, trying to push a boar past a companion. The first day they saw nothing. But the second day, nine of the animals ran past Magnus. "At full speed, and they CAN run!" he commented.

Standers are advised to get off the ground at least four feet, he added. "So the boars can't get at you!"

The boars proved to be tough adversaries. "They have a shield across their back and rib cage that's like cartilage," he continued. "You can't stick an arrow through it. The best shot is one going away where the arrow enters behind the rib cage."

The group found that they had to use different arrows than are used for deer. "We used the old-fashioned broadheads," Mortier said.

"The excitement starts after you shoot one," Hoyt noted. "They'll either come right at you then, or they'll run off into dense cover and turn to face you, and then they come at you!"

"Minnows and Shotgun Shells"

The hunters were accompanied by guides armed with rifles to provide protection. Tracking dogs are also used to recover wounded animals.

Still Mortier had a particularly close call from a wounded boar, even after the guide had shot it in an attempt to finish the animal.

"I shot my arrow," he said. "And the next thing I knew I was looking at a 400-pound pig. I went up a tree about 12 feet!"

In the fight that followed, one of the tracking dogs sustained a deep gash from the boar's sharp tusks.

"I treated the dog to a steak that night at a restaurant!" Mortier said.

The three plan to go back again this November.

An Iowa hunting preserve license and habitat stamp are required. The total cost of the trip runs about $1,000; which includes lodging, one boar, meat processing and a head mount. Hunter numbers are carefully controlled to maintain a high quality experience.

"It's as close as you can get to a wild hunt without going to the southern states," Mortier said. "The wild boar is totally unpredictable."

... That's why they're called the poor man's grizzly!

September, 1999

Lady Summer Bids Good-Bye

Lady Summer and I had a date to keep. There she was, her bags packed and ready to go, anxious to meet up with another of my old girlfriends, Miz Spring. The two would rendezvous down around the Gulf of Mexico, the Lady thought. Down where the porpoises splash and the pouch-billed pelicans perch. There they'd loaf for the next six months, she said, while I shiver here in our frozen north.

Anxious as she was to get going, she'd agreed to stick around for a final day, the last day of the trout season. And to spend it with me on a lonely brush-lined creek.

The day has become a tradition of sorts with us. It marks the end of a special time for me. And when that day is done, I'm ready to lay down the fishing pole and pick up the shotgun.

We met out by the crick, the Lady and I. Overhead hung a leaden, cloud-covered sky. Out of the northeast, a cool breeze blew, one that carried a hint of Lake Superior on its breath. And the Lady grimaced. This was not her thing. She'd best be soon on her way. she seemed to be saying.

I slipped into my waders, and strapped on my old willow wicker-woven creel. And in a last minute concession to the bite in the air, from the back of the pickup, I dug out an old chamois shirt, one that waits there, crumpled and musty, for

"Summer ended with these trout"

just such emergencies.

The walk to the creek took only a few minutes, past fading sheaves of goldenrod and browning marsh grass. Through the alders, their crowns already half-thinned of leaves, I could see the stream, shining like a band of burnished silver as it flowed.

And it was high, bankfull and more! I knew the water would be up. The late-September downpours had put all the streams well above their banks. But that was ten days earlier, and I thought they'd returned to near their normal levels.

Not so, I found, as I stepped into the water. Where knee-deep depths had been the rule all summer, suddenly I found myself waist-deep. And the current had power. A trip, a misstep, a loss of balance, and I'd find myself flat on my backside, I told myself.

But fish I would. After all, it was the last day of the season, my final chance to cavort a bit with my lady friend.

Cautiously, I worked my way upstream, one step at a time, reading the bottom with my booted feet. And the first trout. From the base of a run where the stream bends its way around a little brushy island. A nice eleven-inch brown, golden and fat, one for the creel.

As I continued my wading, I soon learned that "reading" the stream was impossible. The water was too deep. And I fished by instinct, guessing where a spot might hold a fish.

I soon found that the small brook trout were feeding. Small fish are like little kids, always hungry. An hour's fishing produced a dozen or so, with a few large enough to keep.

But the bigger trout, where were they? Had they previously fed and were taking it easy? Around a bend, I tiptoed, skirting the edge of a deep pool, the muck and mire sucking at my boots. And the first nice brookie, a foot-long male

"Minnows and Shotgun Shells"

with white-tipped fins and a belly as orange as a morning sunrise.

And a twin just upstream, where the current curled hard against a steep, marsh grass-draped bank. Another male, bright-colored, its gun-metal blue sides speckled with yellow and violet.

Two nice trout. But that was all. And ever so slowly, I eased my way upstream to better bottom. The hard sand and gravel felt like pavement under my feet.

My last three fish came from a deep hole where the creek's current rampaged its way around a sharp bend. And the best fish of the day, a heavy-bodied foot-plus female brookie, a trout that fought doggedly in the swift water. A fine fish, one on which the season could rightly close. A special fish that will fuel the dreams of winter nights, when the snow lies deep in the backyard.

Lady Summer was waiting for me, her back turned to the brisk breeze, as I climbed up the bank. Together we hiked the half-mile back to the truck.

There we whispered our good-byes.

And then she was gone, leaving me with only fleeting memories of her... and my trout fishing season.

October, 1994

My Friend Bill

There's a tree stand leaning against a tall white oak out at the tree farm these days. It's well-built, made to last, constructed of sturdy lumber. Ten feet skyward, it's ladder extends; and there at its top is a platform, a square where a deer hunter could stand, to silently wait for a big buck to sneak past.

Down the ridge a half a forty or so, is my own seat, faded old boards nailed to three maples. There, if I leaned back and kinked my neck just right, I could pick out through the trees a tiny bit of blaze orange, the coat of the hunter perched on that tree stand to the east.

Not this year, though... not this year. This year the stand will be empty, unoccupied. And my eyes will search in vain for a tiny bit of blaze orange.

The tree stand, you see, belonged to Bill Barton, one of my closest friends... and a close friend to many others. Barton died on August 15 of cancer, a disease that he fought gallantly to overcome, enduring for more than two years the surgeries and radiation treatments that we all prayed would keep him with us. He was only 64.

Barton and I spent a lot of time together. We shared a lot of experiences, some of which appeared in this column over the years. Never have I known a finer man.

"Minnows and Shotgun Shells"

"He was a man of great generosity. He gave of himself to his family, his community, and his church," so Father Gregory Hopefl, pastor of St. Philips church in Stone Lake, eulogized Barton at the funeral service. And I'm certain that none of the 400 people in attendance disagreed. For Bill was a giver. Let there be a need to plow the snow at the church, and there he'd be with his truck. Or cook bratwursts at a local Lions Club fundraiser, and there, dressed in his white apron, he'd be lending his hand.

He was a rare man. I got to know him well, first in our working days when we both were Department of Natural Resources employees, later in our retirement years. For thirty years he was a conservation warden, moving up in the ranks from field stations to supervisory positions. The last twelve years of his career, he led the law enforcement program for the west-central part of Wisconsin from DNR's district headquarters at Eau Claire.

The job required strong leadership ability. Barton had that, both on the job and off. Get a group of people together, and there at its center you'd usually find Bill.

And I learned why, as in recent years we spent more and more time together... many times just the two of us in boats, in ice-fishing shanties, in cabs of pickup trucks as we travelled.

He was a very secure individual, one of great integrity, I learned. An integrity that stemmed from the strength of the personal beliefs, both moral and spiritual, that laid deep within him. He possessed a strong sense of right and wrong, and when his judgement required, he never wavered from those standards. Still, when the time came for healing, he was quick to be fair and forgiving.

Barton truly loved people. Put him anywhere and he was

My Friend Bill

at home, quickly making friends. A story was told to me at the funeral by a couple who travelled south in winters with Bill and Ev Barton, sharing campgrounds. "Bill knew everybody," they said. "We'd go for walks together, but we never got very far because Bill always had so many people to visit with!"

Barton loved to fish, for perch especially. Over the years, a close-knit group of us formed, guys like Joe Zanter, Al Spindler, Joe Rubesch, Larry Keith, and others. Together we fished lakes like Big Winnibigoshish in northern Minnesota and Whitefish in Ontario.

The occasions were truly memorable, cabins rocking with laughter, and venison cook-outs on the ice of wind-swept lakes. There Barton would be at his best. There one frigid January day on Big Winnie, when the temperature was below zero and I was chilled to the bone, I listened as Bill lectured the group of us on the finer points of perch fishing.

"You gotta get those baits right down on the bottom, stir up a little mud with 'em! Chartreuse is the best color," he'd say, as he'd reel in fat fish after fat fish. His manner reminded me of some of my old college profs. And I nicknamed him "Professor Perch."

… No matter that the same day, he allowed his ice auger to freeze so tight in a slush-filled hole that it took the bunch of us an hour to break it free. We loved the guy.

A second comment was passed to me the other day at Barton's funeral. "There's a new angel up in heaven now," the man said, pausing a moment. "And his name is Professor Perch."

Lucky are the rest of the angels, I say.

September, 1995

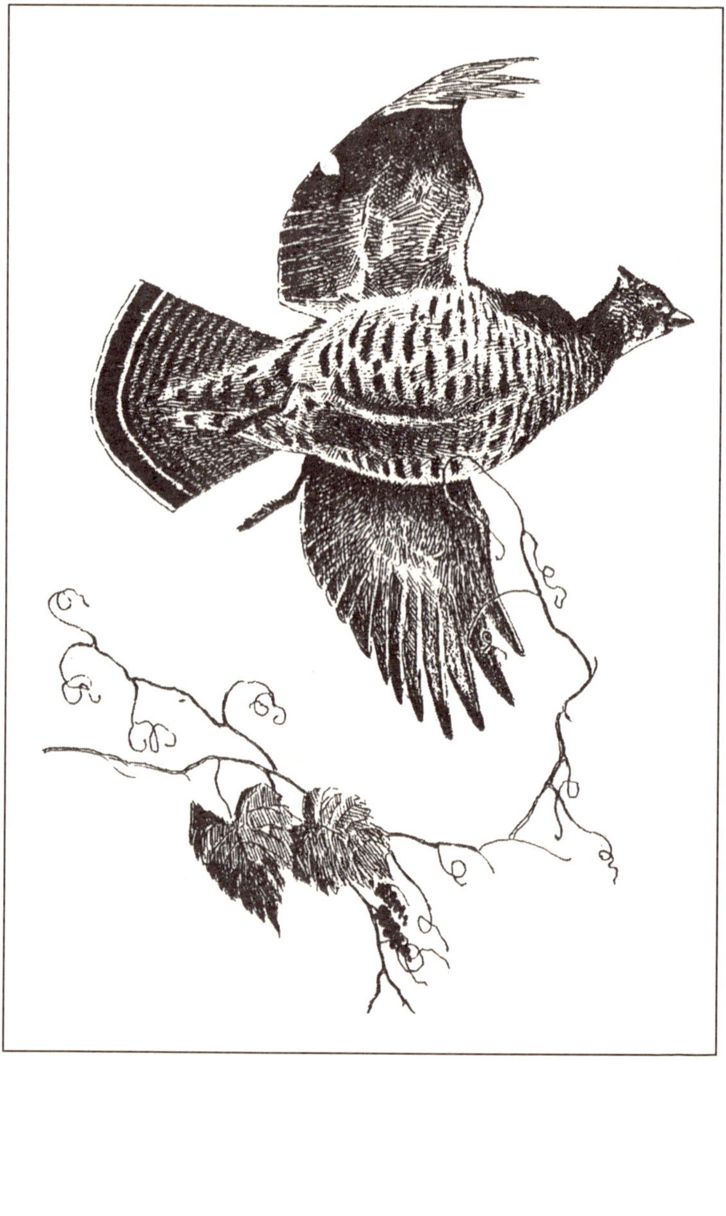

A Hunger For Hunting

Many years ago, when I was a youngster, sometimes one of us kids would fail to clean our plate at supper time. Food was precious, and the guilty one would be chided to finish his meal.

"Your appetite is bigger than your stomach!" my parents would announce.

That scenario came back to me the other evening as I and my faithful, but somewhat over-confident hunting dog, Butch, returned from our first try at the ruffed grouse. My thoughts were not, however, about his appetite for food, though that is substantial, but rather, about his appetite for hunting.

The hunt had been in the making for better than a week. Not only was I psyching myself up, but I also worked on good old Butch, letting him sniff the game pocket of my hunting coat and the shotgun.

"Wanna go get the birds, Butch? Wanna ride in the truck?" I'd wheedle the poor guy, until he was almost beside himself with excitement. Around the house he'd pace, ears cocked, whining, groaning, until Momma would lay the law down to both of us.

"Get out of here and take that poor dog hunting!" she'd order. Which was better than being told to take down the screens or rake the leaves, I figured.

And the time finally arrived the other afternoon. Butch knew what was going on. With one bound from the driveway, he landed on his spot on the pickup seat, there to await my own preparations, confused as they usually are the first trip of the year.

Like suddenly realizing, as I'm about to back out of the driveway, that I didn't have a watch with me. I gave up wearing a watch back in 1985 when I retired! But hunting hours have to be observed to stay legal! So back to the house I had to go.

A half-hour later, found me parking alongside a remote gravel road. Nearby an old logging trail led into the woods. Butch shivered with anticipation as I gathered up my gear: coat, gun, shells, compass, whistle. And finally to him, my "Go get 'em!"

Out the door and into the ferns and brush, he bounded, smashing and crashing... pausing only to mark up a milepost or two, messages he leaves to tell other dogs he's passed that way. I follow behind, picking my way around mudholes, letting old Butch blow off a little steam before he settles down for some serious hunting. Which takes a quarter-mile or so.

Quietly we sneak along the old road, through the blackberry brush, now turning bronze, and the hazel thickets that line its edges. Beyond lies a sea of young aspen trees, thick, almost impenetrable, good grouse cover.

At least it was in years past, times when the bird's cycle was up, and flushes came easy. Did the habitat produce this year, I wondered, as I poked along. Up ahead, staying nicely in shotgun range, Butch prowled, sniffing the ground for scent, exploring the cover.

VAROOM! The grouse exploded from the popple some

A Hunger For Hunting

20 yards off the trail. Time for only a quick 'snap' shot. And into the woods, Butch and I waded to see if I'd connected. Five minutes of searching with his experienced nose turned up nothing. A clean miss!

And on we move, optimistic that there'd be more chances. Such was not the case, however. Four hours of hunting turned up not another grouse.

Through the network of old trails we hunted. Past places where birds once fell. Past the spot where Butch made his first retrieve. Through the old log landing, now growing up, to where we once treed a fisher. Past the oak tree where the big weasel-like animal climbed to look down at us, contempt in its eyes.

Past our 'sittin' logs, places where we pause to rest, where Butch crowds tight against my booted feet, as I drink in the beauty of the autumn woods around us.

And finally the long hike back. My old legs are beginning to tire, and Butch goes about his business more slowly, more matter-of-factly.

By the time we reach the pickup, we've covered three miles, plenty for the first hunt of the year. And we're both dragging.

At home, I open the back door and Butch drags himself inside, hobbling slowly across the kitchen, limping on a front leg, to flop himself down in front of the furnace register.

Momma looks him over in silence, then shakes her head, and says, "He's a mess!"

And she's right. The old boy's appetite for hunting had been bigger than his stomach.

He'd bitten off more than he could chew!

October, 1996

A Fishing Season Ends

The summer fishing season came to an end the other day. By summer, I mean my open water fishing. As versus ice fishing. Which is just around the corner.

The season ended on a fitting note, on a beautiful northern Wisconsin fall morning.

I dumped Big Al, my boat, into a little lake, one that I'd been meaning to fish all summer. Years back, I made many a trip to it. But in recent times, for some vague reason, I hadn't tried the little gem.

The lake has had a reputation of being a pretty good walleye lake. And I'd found that to be true in the past. No, I never came home with a limit from those outings. But a trip was usually good for two or three keepers in an afternoon. And nice eating-size fish.

Perhaps a hundred or so acres, the lake's not hard to learn. A couple of slow passes over it with the depth-finder is all one needs to get a good picture of its bottom... where the weed beds grow, where the drop-offs occur. So, it's easy to fish.

The nicest thing about the lake, however, is its solitude. Particularly in September and October, when the boat traffic drops. That's when I'd go there. That's when I'd settle back on a nice soft boat cushion, prop my feet up on the gunwale,

A Fishing Season Ends

and cast my jigs and minnows for the walleyes that prowled below.

That's what happened the other day.

A Sunday morning, the world was quiet. Into a cloudless, blue sky overhead, the sun was climbing over the wooded eastern shoreline, its warmth slowly seeping into my insulated float coat.

A whisper of a breeze barely dimpled the water's surface. Not good walleye fishing conditions, I told myself. The bright sunshine would penetrate deep in the clear water. Walleyes don't like bright sunshine.

But hope springs eternal in the hearts of old walleye fishermen, and I positioned Big Al for a slow drift across a familiar stretch of sandy bottom interspersed with submerged water weeds, stringy green stuff now dying and rotting. The vegetation would offer some underwater shade, cover that might hold a hungry walleye.

And the sounds of early morning, of the world coming to life, began to drift across the lake. Voices. A human speaking at one of the cottages. Crows and blue jays calling. The shrieks of white gulls as they circled. A lawn mower sputtering as someone mulched leaves. A chain saw growling in the distance. Firewood-cutting probably.

The first fish came some half-way across the lake. I felt it tap my minnow, gave it a few seconds to mouth the bait, then set the hook. From its first rush, I figured it wasn't a walleye, and I was right.

A large-mouth bass! My first glimpse of the critter told me so... its chunky body, the black stripe on its sides. Two pounds, I guessed, as I unhooked the fish, and dropped it back into the lake.

Then, more sounds of the morning! The best part of the

"Minnows and Shotgun Shells"

day, as a matter of fact.

From the north, came the shrill gabble of geese. There, still only specks in the sky, in a wave, they came. Five separate, distinct flocks! A good 500 of the magnificent birds, I estimated.

What a sight, as they approached! What a sound as they passed! What a privilege to be there with them!

And a second fish, this time one that hit and fought with more authority. A northern pike, I soon saw, as it flashed under the boat. But a decent fish, one worth keeping.

A perfect northern, I say, is one of about 22 inches. It fillets well, cooks nicely and tastes sweet and succulent. And into the live well it went.

That's the way the morning passed. Back and forth over the weedbeds and bars I moved. A gentle breeze arose, putting a nice chop on the water, raising my hopes that the walleyes, if they're still there, would begin to feed.

But that was not to be. A second respectable northern joined the one in the live well. As did a nice crappie. And a third northern released. But no walleyes.

Quitting time came in early afternoon. The last fishing trip for the summer had been a good one, an appropriate climax. I'd take Big Al home, strip him of his batteries and other gear, and tuck my good pal away for the winter.

Like the geese that had passed overhead, the time had come for the both of us to move on.

November, 1999

A Good Grouse Day For Butch

Zigging instead of zagging again!

That was the thought crossing my mind as I headed out for an afternoon of grouse hunting. Outside the truck, however, hung a picture-perfect Indian Summer day... a day tailor-made for walleye fishing; warm, sunny, drowsy, tempting.

Beside me, excited in anticipation, sat my long-time hunting dog companion, Butch. Butch was the main reason I was going hunting instead of fishing.

The Old Boy, you see, had been threatening to run away from home.

"Fishing! Shmishing!" he'd barked at me out at his kennel. "Enough is enough! What am I around here, some kind of a fifth wheel? When do I get some attention?"

What he was saying, of course, was the fact that the ruffed grouse season had been open for over a month. But we had yet to go hunting. And my fever for fall fishing was a reason.

The guilt hit me.

"You got a point, old buddy?" I told him. "Tomorrow we'll try the grouse."

And there'd been a couple of other reasons why we hadn't hunted.

October is Christmas tree tagging time. And having been

"Minnows and Shotgun Shells"

indoctrinated from early age on to the ethic that business comes before pleasure, the better part of two weeks had been spent out at the Tree Farm stapling red tags onto spruces and balsams... getting them ready for the harvest season that lies just ahead.

And lastly, a personal prejudice, namely that I don't like to hunt when the trees and brush are still coated with leaves. I prefer to wait until they're down, to when the woods opens up.

But the Christmas tree tagging was done, and most of the leaves had fallen. The time had come to take the shotgun out of its case... to give Butch his due.

We'd hunt the trails on our Tree Farm. The 160 acres is more than Christmas trees. The forest is also a mix of maple and oak, stands which have been selectively thinned by logging over time, trees that now stand straight and healthy. And aspen and white birch patches, groves which we've clearcut in the past that now have reproduced to dense thickets of young trees, the kind of cover that ruffed grouse love.

Along the woods road, Butch and I sneaked; I pussy-footing quietly, Butch exploring the blackberry and hazel brush that flanks the trail.

A quarter mile and the first bird. It rose from the thick cover on my right, quartering away from me. The old shooting instincts of the past returned as I swung on the grouse. At the shot, it dropped, and I marked it down. No need to, however. Butch was there well before me.

And I praised him and complimented myself. A good start.

Onward the two of us poked, I admiring how fast the red oaks were growing with one eye, and watching Butch with the other. And a stylish point in the shady side of the young

A Good Grouse Day For Butch

aspen. There Butch stood, frozen, eyes and nose fixed forward.

Slowly, I eased ahead, expecting the flush. With a thunder of wings the bird rose... right into the afternoon sun. And I shot. Not too confidently, however. And for several minutes, Butch and I searched for it in vain.

"Nope, Boss! You missed that one," he seemed to tell me, as he displayed little interest in the search.

In a little valley, where the trail curves, young aspen on one side, and big oak on the other, a second fancy point. Two birds this time. And smart cusses too. Because both streaked away, putting trees between me and them before I could pull a trigger.

That's the way the afternoon passed. In all, we raised eight grouse. Of course, five escaped without a shot being fired. Of the three others, only the one bounced in the back pocket of my hunting coat at the end of the day.

And that's the way it's supposed to be. It's called fair chase. Over the 45-some years I've hunted, by far more grouse have escaped me than I've bagged.

What's important is to enjoy the hunt, I say. The day in the wild, a faithful dog who loves his job, and the matching of wits with the finest of all game birds.

As we headed home, Butch laid curled beside me on the seat of the truck; asleep, tired... his nose nestled against the cased shotgun. He'd had a good day.

I was glad I'd zigged instead of zagged.

November, 1998

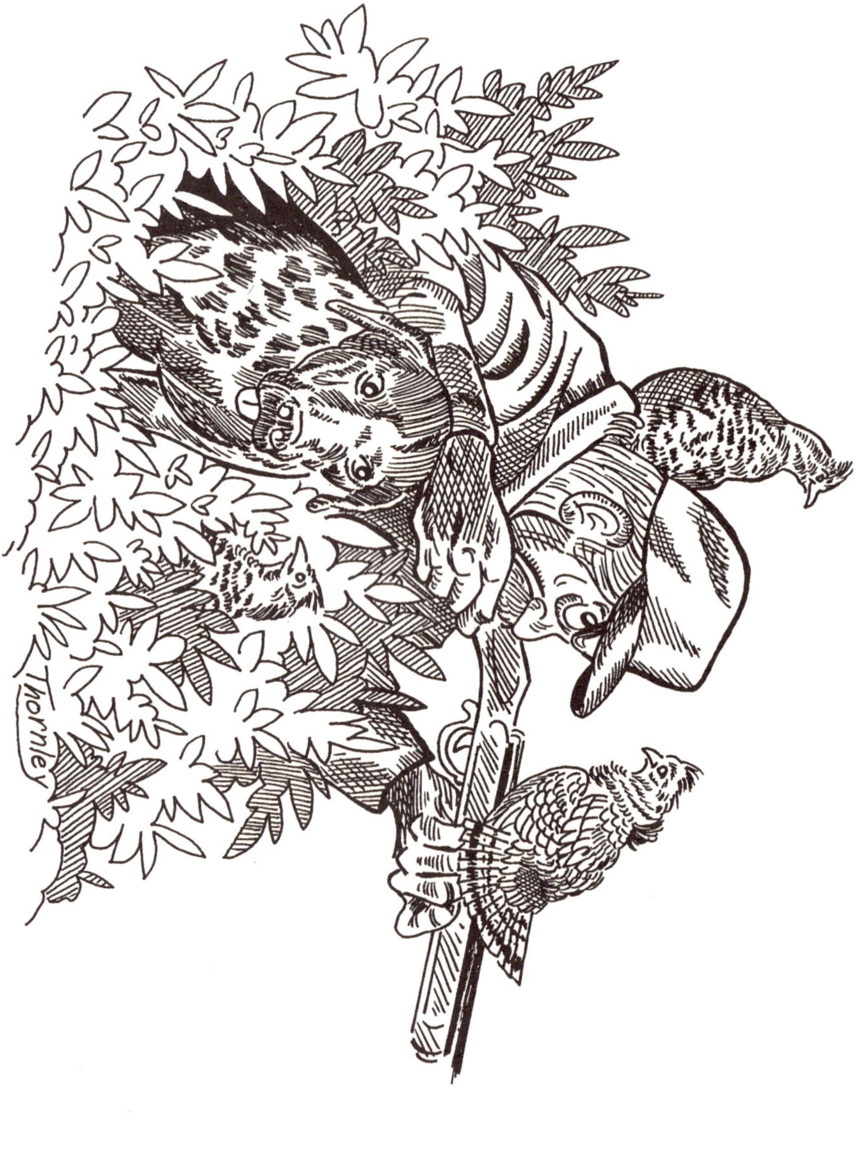
Thornley

Grouse Keep Getting Sneakier

I swear, our ruffed grouse are getting sneakier every year. The critters have always been known for their dirty tricks. But the last few years, they seem to be out-doing themselves. I got to thinking about that the other day, after a walk around some of the tree farm trails. Are the birds getting smarter, I asked myself, or am I just getting dumber? (After meditating on that point for a minute or two, I decided I really didn't want an answer.)

Old Ruff and I have been crossing hunting paths for some forty years now. And to his credit, I have to say he's America's finest game bird. We've had a lot of fun trying to outwit each other.

But the last few years, it seems, the outwitting is all one-sided. Old Ruff is the out-witter and I'm the out-wittee!

I can't remember the last time I had an easy shot at a grouse! Used to be that there'd always be a dummy or two that would get up and fly right down the middle of the trail!

Not any more! I swear we've evolved a super bird, a super grouse. One with an IQ that exceeds mine. Which doesn't take much evolving, I realize.

Take the other day, for instance.

Butch, my German shorthair hunting partner, and I had been out to the tree farm all day tagging Christmas trees, getting the green-needled beauties lined up for the coming harvest season.

Well, at quitting time, tired, I packed it in, and Butch and I headed home, slowly driving the bumpy trail through the pines. There, off the road a bit in the Norways, stood a grouse... boldly, brazenly eyeing the truck. Like I was some kind of an intruder on its property. And get off!

That's the kind of personality our grouse are developing! And me with no gun along!

Well, I stopped, quietly opened the door, and let Butch out. About two steps, and he froze into one of his classic three-point poses. Like one of those big Green Bay Packer linemen.

Well, the grouse just chuckled a couple of good clucks, walked away, and with a final insult cluck, flushed deeper into the pines.

Needless to say, the whole episode got me a bit perturbed. I'm happy to have grouse living on my land. But I don't particularly appreciate them sticking their tongues out at me!

"Butch," I said, "it's time we put these foul-minded fowls in their place!"

And a couple days later, back to the tree farm we went. This time with the shotgun under my arm... ready for action.

(Remember now what I said earlier about grouse getting sneakier!)

Along one of the trails, Butch and I pussy-footed. Butch checking the back corners of the cover, I taking the easy going, walking the trail.

Past the spruce plantation, the outside row of which is now 40-feet tall... planted by Momma on a hot, dusty April day back in 1969.

Back along the ridge, through the oaks that now have

Grouse Keep Getting Sneakier

grown into tall, straight high-quality trees.

Around the loop trail we circled, through the thick 30-year-old popples that are rapidly approaching another harvest.

Nothing. No birds.

And as we reached the spruce plantation once more, there in the grass laid an empty soda pop can, a souvenir left by a benevolent trespasser. And I bent over to pick it up.

That's when a grouse flew up! As I was crumpling the pop can and stuffing it into my hunting coat pocket!

One hasty futile shot. I missed, of course.

And that's when two more flew out of the top of the spruce… one just a blur through the green foliage, the other swooping down low over my head, almost taking my cap off!

Well, there I am, making like a ballerina! Two more futile shots as the bird dodged and wove through the popples, laughing I'm sure.

And as I opened my gun, to re-load, another from the spruce tree top!

See what I mean? See what I'm talking about? Talk about nasty! Talk about sneaky!

I'm telling you, we've got a rotten, inconsiderate, obnoxious breed of grouse on our hands.

Something's got to be done about it!

… Next hunting trip. (Maybe!)

October, 1999

Fall Walleye Memories

The big buck had pretty much said it all.

The handsome animal had crossed the road ahead of us. And I slowed the pickup as we approached the spot. There he stood, his eight-point rack held high, steam streaming in the cold air from his nostrils. Then, oblivious to us, with his nose to the ground, he trotted slowly away through the pine trees.

His behavior was typical of his kind in early November... a time when bucks throw caution to the winds, as they engage in their annual rutting, or breeding, season. Obviously, that was what the critter was up to, on the trail of a doe.

The deer had made kind of a statement with me. Perhaps I, and my partners, should be getting ready for the deer season... not trailing boats behind our pickups, heading for a boat landing a few miles up the road.

But, just as the buck had important things on its mind, so did we. Only our love affair was with walleyes, fish that we'd come to the Boulder Junction area of Vilas County to court.

True, we'd come to catch fish. Yet, there'd been a second reason, one that dealt with a different kind of love, feelings that we harbored deep within our hearts for an old friend.

Fall Walleye Memories

His name was Tom Newcomb, a fisherman and guide so good and so well-regarded in his trade, that he was enshrined in the Fishing Hall of Fame at Hayward after his death from a heart attack in 1993.

I came to know Newcomb through Johnny Walker, a guy with whom I fish a lot. Walker and Newcomb were high school classmates, and in later years, fellow guides.

Each year, Newcomb would organize one last fling of walleye fishing in November. As he put it, "You're not really a walleye fisherman unless you fish the week before deer season!"

And each year, he'd invite a bunch of us to his cabin on Rice Creek. There we'd hole up, talk smart, and close the summer fishing season. Always, the weather was brutal, cold, often windy. Many times ice had to be broken to get the boats to open water.

The get-togethers are now a thing of the past. Still, the tradition lives on. This fall, Walker organized some of us from the old gang to gather for that final fling. And though we stayed in a motel, not Newcomb's cabin, we came for the same reason, for the fishing... and to remember Tom.

This year, there were five of us: Walker and I; Bob Speich of Hayward; Tom Kullman, another longtime Newcomb friend; and Myk Hensley, of Boulder Junction, a rugged young man who knows the Vilas County back country like the back of his hand.

For parts of the three days we fished the Spider-Island Lake chain, concentrating on the bay-and-bar waters that Newcomb had known so well. Clad in insulated coats and snowmobile suits, with gloved hands working our reels, we cast our minnow-baited jigs.

We caught fish. One day of the three the walleyes cooper-

"Minnows and Shotgun Shells"

ated, the other two they didn't. But what the fish lacked in numbers, they made up for in size, chunky and heavy-shouldered. The fish averaged between three and four pounds, a very nice run of walleyes.

Fishing trips are more than fish, however. The shorelunch, for instance, that Myk Hensley cooked for us was something special. It'd been awhile since I'd enjoyed the luxurious aroma of wood smoke curling skyward, spiced with the fragrance of frying potatoes. And there were the chuckles as Kullman tied into a "big one," only to land an ancient rod and reel that had gone over the side of someone's boat long ago.

Eagles soared over the pine-covered shorelines and mallards sped high overhead. White gulls circled our boats waiting for dead minnows to be cast aside, and loons dove, surfacing with fish in their beaks.

And over it all, hung the spirit of Tommy Newcomb.

Several times, I gazed up the marshy mouth of Rice Creek toward his cabin, reliving my memories of the man.

He was there, I'm sure. I just couldn't see him.

November, 1997

A Quality Called Courage

Today's story is about deer hunting… about a little seven-point buck that was shot recently, and about the young man that bagged it.

On the surface, the story may appear typical of many hunts going on around our northwoods these days. The bow season's open, and a fair number of deer are being taken by archers.

The story, however, has another side to it, a special side… one that carries a powerful message about an intangible something called courage.

First, the hunter.

His name is Craig Simpson, a personable young man of 32. He lives in Plymouth, Minnesota, though he's spent much of his lifetime in Wisconsin. His folks, Martin and Joan, own and operate a large farm near Trego in Washburn County.

There, amid the rolling fields and hardwood hills, Craig grew up, acquiring as he did, a deep love for the outdoors, especially deer hunting.

"I've been bow hunting since I was twelve," he told me recently. "I shot my first buck when I was 16, an eight pointer. I shot 21 bucks with bow and gun by the time I was 26. Of course, I hunted in two states, Wisconsin and

"Disabled Craig Simpson continues to hunt deer"

A Quality Called Courage

Minnesota."

But then a fateful day in February of 1992... a car accident on the way home from work in Minnesota.

"Life was going good," he said. "I had a good job. I was married, and had a new home."

The accident left him a quadriplegic... changing his life drastically.

"But you go on," he said. "You keep on truckin'! I wanted to keep on enjoying the outdoors. My love for the outdoors was a strong motivator for me to go on with life.

"I've become very independent for my level of injury," he added. "I drive, and I'm going to school for computer graphics. I try to come home every other weekend, except in the winter."

This fall, he's made several trips home to bow hunt on the family farm. Because he's disabled, he qualifies for a special permit issued by the DNR to shoot from a stationary vehicle.

"I have a couple of ground blinds built in our woods with camouflage netting around them," Craig told. "So I can drive my four-wheeler right in. One is on the top of a hill, so I'm looking down. The deer pass through, feeding on acorns, to our hay field. But you can't hunt the field because the deer don't get there until after shooting time is over."

Simpson hunts with a crossbow, a spring-loaded weapon that shoots a short arrow-like "bolt." The bow has been modified so that he can fire it with a mouthpiece.

"I have a friend who has a machine shop, who did the modification," he explained.

He requires help to cock the crossbow, however. "Dad or Mom help me cock it," he said. "It's a team effort. I'm very fortunate that they're willing to help. I carry a cellular phone with me, so I can call home if I get a deer.

"Minnows and Shotgun Shells"

"The first night out, I passed up a six-pointer and a fork-horn," he told. "I'm limited to one shot, that's all I get. And I passed up the deer because they weren't good clean shots."

And on a recent late afternoon... his big moment.

"The buck was just moseying through, walking upwind. I shot when it was about 25 yards away. I saw in my scope where the arrow hit the deer. I called home on my phone, and both Mom and Dad came out. We found the deer a short distance from where I'd shot it."

The deer was destined for processing when I visited the Simpsons the next day. Craig likes venison, and the meat would be going back with him to his Minnesota home.

"I won't let it go to waste," he said. "The horns will go on a plaque. It's the first buck I've shot since I was disabled."

He'll continue to hunt in Minnesota, he noted. There he belongs to two organizations that offer opportunities for disabled people to hunt and fish, the United Foundation for Disabled Archers, and Capable Partners.

And therein lies the mighty message about courage. Courage that provides the will and the determination for Craig Simpson to go on with his life. Courage that in his case is fueled by a deep love for the outdoors.

"Sometimes when I'm hunting, my best enjoyment is having a fawn eating acorns only 15 feet away from me," he told me from his wheelchair the other day. "Or a porcupine climbing a tree next to me. Or the raccoons, foxes, and grouse that I see."

Courage that helps him keep on truckin' with life.

October, 1997

Deer Hunting Wasn't Lady-Like

Deer hunting wasn't considered lady-like when Dorie Brunner was growing up at Medford in the 1930's. "All my uncles and my grandfather on the mother's side were deer hunters," she tells. "But my parents were against my going. 'Dorie, don't do that,' they'd say."

Nevertheless, that didn't stop her from pursuing the sport. "I begged my grandfather to take me," she said. "My first hunt was in 1940 when I was 14.

"We went up to the Loretta-Draper area where my uncles were logging. I didn't know beans about hunting," she added. "My grandfather put me on a stump and said, 'now you stay here.' I used an old 38-40 octagon-barrel rifle. The bullet was so big and slow you could actually see it in the air when you fired!"

Brunner never saw a deer that first hunt. "There weren't many deer back then," she said. "And there weren't many hunters to move them."

In the 55 seasons since, however, the rural Barron County resident has had excellent success. She's bagged 42 deer in that time, a record that not many hunters can match.

"I didn't go last season," she said. "I'd had surgery on my shoulder, and I couldn't get my rifle up."

She's seen a lot of changes in Wisconsin deer hunting.

Outdoor clothing is an example. When she first hunted, she wore knickers. "I almost froze to death! You didn't have the good clothing we have today," she said.

Guns are better too, she explains. She's owned several, a 30-30 bolt action and a carbine, both of which served her well. Her favorite today, however, is a .284 caliber Winchester.

Besides the Loretta area, she's hunted near Tomahawk, Perkinstown and Superior. "There I got lost in a big swamp," she said.

And she's hunted in California and Canada, where her party bagged a moose and caught "umpteen walleyes."

Perhaps her most unusual hunt, however, took place in 1951 in Germany. A physical education teacher by profession, Brunner had accepted a job with the U.S. Army as a recreation director.

"I wanted to go deer hunting and our commanding officer found me a .30 caliber Army carbine," she told. "You had to hunt with a guide who is called a 'Jaeger.' You pay him and give him some of the meat. The deer are Roe deer. They're small, only about 50 pounds, but I got one."

Her favorite hunting grounds today are the Sand Creek area of Polk County and the Oak Lake area of Washburn County. There she's joined by her daughter, Sarah. Snapshots of bucks they've bagged testify to the hunting abilities of the two.

And some interesting memories... like the time Sarah carried in their rifles in the early morning darkness, only to leave the wrong one with Dorie.

An eight-point rack on the wall tells of a buck Dorie once shot. "I had it all gutted-out when I slipped and went up to my elbow into its body cavity. I had to walk down to a creek to wash my arm, and I took off my watch. When I got back to the deer, I discovered I'd forgotten the watch, and I had to go back again. It took me two hours to get that deer taken care of!

"Five years ago I heard a crash-crash and here comes a bear not ten feet from me! Another time a fawn came so close that I patted it on the rump!"

Brunner has her own techniques for hunting. "I'm a sitter," she says. "I have patience. I scrape all the leaves away from my stand, and I won't sit where I'm silhouetted against the sky. I won't shoot at a deer unless I know that I'll put it down!"

Nothing of her deer is wasted. One year recently, a meat market processed her deer at no charge, a compliment to her for how well it had been taken care of.

"My three Huskie dogs get the liver and birds get the tallow," she said. "And I make buttons and bolo ties from the horns."

Dorie Brunner told me a lot more the other day about her love for the outdoors as we visited, while snowflakes danced outside the windows. Things like her fishing, her grouse and duck hunting and her skiing.

And how she and a girl friend, back in 1960, canoed the Mississippi River from Bemidji, Minnesota to New Orleans, a two-month adventure, camping out as they paddled.

Now 70 years old, she plans to be back on one of her lucky deer stands when the season arrives this year. "But maybe not in 1997," she says. "It's getting harder to go. What used to be fun-fun is getting to be work!"

Fifty-six seasons is a lot of deer hunting!

Good luck, Dorie… may 1996 be your best hunt ever!

November, 1996

An Impossible Dream Comes True

Can an impossible dream become a reality? It can... just ask Bob Volz.

Volz, 47, lives in Minong. There he's owned and operated a thriving trucking business since 1982. His trucks haul pulpwood for the Mosinee Paper Company from its lands in the area, and turkey meat products for the Jerome Foods company of Barron, delivering the food to 48 states and Mexico.

As a boy, Volz grew up in Spooner, acquiring as he did, a deep love for the outdoors, of hunting and fishing.

"As a little boy, I was intrigued by the stories Bill Stewart used to write in the Spooner paper about his elk hunting trips out west," he told.'

But sometimes boyhood dreams are shattered, only to fade in adult life. And that appeared to happen for Volz on a fateful day in 1987, ten years ago.

That day, Bob was working in his shop, installing a furnace. "I fell off a ladder and hurt my back," he said. "Fortunately, my 13-year-old son was with me. He went and got help. He saved my life."

The accident left Volz a paraplegic, wheelchair-bound.

"I was in the hospital two months," he explained. "One day, I said 'I'm going home and going back to work.' And I

An Impossible Dream Comes True

discharged myself.

"Basically, I went on with my life," he continued. "I'm one of those guys who has to be doing something. I knew no one was going to hand me anything. I had a family, a wife and two sons. My wife, Judy, has been very supportive. My entire family has been very good to me!"

Today, Volz lives an active life. "I drive a pickup, cut my own lawn, run a Skidster," he said.

His accident, however, put an end to his hunting. Until a few weeks ago, that is, when he was invited to join a group for an elk hunting trip to New Mexico.

"I hadn't done any big game hunting since I was hurt," he said. "But that trip was a good time!"

The group, five hunters and one non-hunter, hunted near Cimarron on a large private ranch.

"We stayed in an old miner's cabin in a ghost town," Volz said. "The ranch is the largest family-owned cattle ranch in New Mexico, over 50,000 acres. Each of us hunters had our own guide, and our camp cook was a cowboy from the ranch."

Volz's four-day license began on a Saturday. "But on Friday, they took us out to a rifle range to test our shooting. I hadn't shot a rifle in ten years, but after a few shots, I was shooting well."

The ranch is located in the foothills of the Rockie Mountains, dry and semi-open country. Long-range shooting is the rule. And for that, Volz chose a bolt action Winchester .270 caliber rifle with a 3 x 9 scope.

The guides strictly control the hunt, picking the bull elk that are to be taken. "I saw nine bulls the first day," Volz said. "One was a 5 by 5 (points on each antler) but the guide said to let it go. Our group shot four 6 by 6 bulls the first two days." The fifth hunter passed up his chance, while looking

"Minnows and Shotgun Shells"

for a 7 by 7 trophy.

Volz brought his bull down with two shots at 350 yards. His first shot took the animal in the front shoulder, and the second put it down to stay.

"It probably weighed 800 pounds," Volz said. "The guide figured the antlers would score about 315 Boone and Crockett points. The head, cape and horns are now being mounted by a taxidermist."

The boned-out meat was packed in coolers and dry ice for the trip home. "It filled a whole freezer," Volz said. "It's better than beef. We're working on it already!"

The group stayed an extra day at the ranch, roaming around. "During our stay, we saw a lot of wild turkeys, more elk, bear, mule and whitetail deer, antelope, and a lot of coyotes," Volz said.

And now his interest in hunting has been revived.

"I've got the bug again," he commented. "I want to go caribou hunting next, and I intend to go back to New Mexico for an antelope hunt. Next fall during the special hunt for disabled people, I'd like to try for a trophy whitetail here in Wisconsin."

Looking back at his New Mexico hunt, Bob Volz says, "It was something you dream a lifetime of doing!"

Which proves that boyhood dreams, even shattered ones, sometimes do come true.

November, 1997

A Hunter For 65 Years

Not many hunters can lay claim to wearing out a deer rifle.

Russell Grandy can. He's worn out two. Now 77, the retired Washburn County farmer has been hunting deer and other game for 65 years.

"I started hunting with a .32 caliber Remington pump," he said. "I wore it out. It's an antique. And I wore out a 742 Remington. I sent it in to the factory, but they said the gun was shot out. They gave me $100 off on a new one!"

Grandy shot his first buck in 1931 when he was 12 years old. "We hunted west of Dairyland in Douglas County," he said. "Deer were very rare around Spooner back then. If a neighbor reported seeing a deer, we'd drive over to see it too.

"It wasn't until the late 1930's and early 1940's that there were many deer around here. From then on the deer population continued to increase to the south. It's hard for people to believe that today."

Grandy remembers some special bucks, like the ten-pointer that he shot in 1945 that's mounted on his living room wall. "I'd driven the deer out to my hunting partner, Conrad Foss, the year before. But he missed it when his gun misfired. The antlers are just two-eighths short of the Boone and Crockett record book."

"Russell Grandy shot his first buck in 1931"

And an eight-pointer that he missed at very close range. "It came right toward me on a logging road," he told. "But I couldn't shoot because I didn't know where my partner was. I stepped into a creek with one foot and that may have thrown my shooting off as the deer went by me."

Grandy feels that today's high deer population doesn't give young hunters an appreciation for hunting. "It's mostly a matter of shooting," he noted. "My idea was to take a track and match wits with the animal. We'd track a buck for hours. Sometimes we'd get a shot, sometimes we wouldn't."

He also stresses safety. "That was always my primary concern, to be sure of what was behind what I was shooting at. I was out there to kill a deer, but safety came first."

Grandy's wife, Betty, was with him on many of his hunts. "She hunted with me many, many years," he said. "She shot antelope and deer with me. But she gave up hunting when she couldn't handle guns anymore... because of arthritis in her hands."

Betty Grandy passed away on July 5, 1996. Russell misses her deeply.

The two travelled west to Wyoming for many years to hunt. "We probably shot 50 antelopes and that many mule deer," he said. "We filled our licenses but that was all."

Two mounts of 14-inch antelope horns tell of trophies they took. "It took three years to bag that one," he said, pointing to one of the mounts. "It doesn't quite make the record book."

Today, Grandy shoots a scope-mounted .243 Remington semi-automatic, a gun that's well suited to the open western country. "If I'd had that gun up along the Namekagon River when I was younger, some of those big bucks up there wouldn't have lived very long," he said. "That used to be

"Minnows and Shotgun Shells"

open country!"

He still owns his first gun, a single-shot .410 shotgun. "It cost $6.98, and I paid for it with weasel hides at 15 cents apiece," he commented. "I remember when 22 shot ammunition was 11 cents a box and shotgun shells were 40 cents a box!

"In 1937 and 1938, I worked at the Lampson store," he added. "We sold 30-30 carbines for $12.00."

Grandy has a deep respect for nature.

"I've really enjoyed my hunting," he said. "You see so many things in the woods, deer sneaking and other birds and animals. I've walked over a good share of Douglas, Burnett and Washburn Counties!"

And wildlife management.

"People should see what happens when deer starve in a deer yard," he commented. "Deer are very mean to one another. The does hit everything in sight, fawns and bucks. It's not like Bambi!"

Game that he brought home was always used for food. "My dad had a saying whenever I'd go fishing or hunting. 'What you bring home you take care of,' he'd say. He was very stern about that. No game was ever brought home and thrown out."

Russell Grandy's love for the outdoors continues to burn deeply within him. He intends to hunt this coming season, though Betty, his wife and hunting partner for the past 51 years, will not be at his side.

"She would want me to go," Russell said.

You can be sure that he'll know that she's there... in thought and spirit.

November, 1996

Montana Elk Guide

Ben Skinner's life, in a sense, has come full circle. Skinner, of rural Siren, has returned to his boyhood roots, to the land of his forefathers.

"There's a lot of history written here," I said to Ben, as he stepped from the door of the snug log home that he and his wife, Marge, have built. Nearby stood a vintage red barn and a gabled farm house, buildings from an era long past.

"My great-grandfather, George Malone, homesteaded this land in the early 1890's," Ben replied. "The house was built in 1896. This was a dairy farm. They raised nine children here.

"My dad worked in Minneapolis, and I was born and raised there," he continued. "But only to go to school. The minute school was out, I was up here!"

There, on the old farm, Skinner learned to hunt and fish. "My dad and uncle were hunters and fishermen," he said. "I got my first fly rod from my dad when I was confirmed."

And that great love for the outdoors became part of his life, remaining strong to the present.

"I enjoy fly fishing for trout," he said. "I don't fish the streams around here much any more. I go mostly out west now. I fish with a friend in Montana. We ride horses up to the timberline and fish mountain streams for cutthroat trout.

"Ben Skinner guided elk hunters in Montana for 18 years"

I do a little walleye fishing around here, and I like to fly-fish for bass and panfish.

"I used to do a lot of duck hunting," he continued. "Two week ago, a buddy and I went to Manitoba to hunt geese. It was a boyhood dream fulfilled!"

Elk hunting, however, has been his first love.

"I always had an urge to go," he said. "I made my first trip to Idaho in 1966. I'd go every other year after that, on seven to ten-day trips. But I found that even that wasn't enough... and I went to work as a guide.

"I guided in Montana for 18 years. One year I put in 52 days in elk camps. There's an early season in places out there that starts around the middle of September. You get about 2 1/2 months of season."

Skinner speaks with authority on elk hunting. "I've got a lot of tent time," he said. "I worked for three outfitters. We were issued permits by the U.S. Forest Service to camp. A typical hunt was 10 days, a one-day horseback ride in, eight days of hunting, and a one-day ride out. All of our equipment and food was packed in on horses."

The parties ranged from four to six hunters. "Then, you needed a guide for every two hunters, a cook... and if you were lucky, a wrangler to take care of the horses.

"I've seen the good years and the bad," he said. "Some years there almost seemed to be a surplus. One time, a hunter I was guiding motioned to me to come over to him. A herd of about 300 elk was in front of him, and he couldn't decide which one to shoot! He shot at two bulls, but he never touched a hair... he was so excited."

Lack of shooting skills, and the physical condition of hunters, were problems. "So many hunters were out of shape for mountain hunting," Skinner said. "They get out there and find that it's harder than they expected.

"And people's life-styles have changed so much. When I first started guiding, hunters didn't expect the luxuries that they do today."

Marge, Ben's wife, also spent time in elk camps as a cook. "I cut my own kindling wood and got our water out of the creek," she told. "It was really fun!"

Ben is a lifetime member of the Rocky Mountain Elk Foundation. The group is concerned over the loss of elk habitat.

"The most stressful time for elk is in the winter," he said. "Their range then is in the valleys, and that's where a lot of land is going into commercial development."

Now retired, Skinner is looking forward to doing more hunting of his own.

"This will be my first year at home," he said. "I've purchased a Wisconsin deer license, and I'm doing some bow hunting. I plan to go mountain goat hunting in Alaska next year. These are some of the things I've wanted to do since I quit guiding."

Skinner is also very interested in hunter safety education, having served as an instructor for 10 years in Minnesota. Currently he is teaching a safety course at Grantsburg.

"It's important to the youngsters," he said. "The course teaches not only safety, but also the ethics of hunting."

Thus, as Ben Skinner learned his hunting values at an early age, that cycle now continues as he passes on his knowledge to present-day youngsters.

A more qualified mentor would be hard to find.

Ben Skinner has seen a lot of hunting situations in his lifetime.

November, 1997

A Half-Century of Deer Hunts

Another deer season is about to dawn. In one respect, it'll be special for me... 1998 will mark my 50th anniversary of Wisconsin deer hunting.

My half-century goes back to 1948. I remember that first season very well. That year, I joined my Uncle Herb on a trip to the Manitowish Waters area of Vilas County.

As a youth, Uncle Herb had been my hunting mentor. Still, I was green as grass about deer hunting. Uncle Herb, however, had gone "up north" a time or two, and he seemed to know the ropes. So when he asked me to join him, I jumped at the opportunity.

I had one small problem to overcome. I was in my first year of college, and I'd have to cut a couple days of classes. Not too smart, but I decided to take the chance. And the Friday before the season, we climbed into Herb's black Plymouth and headed north.

Well, to make a long story short, neither of us got a deer that year. And as I look back, neither of us were much as deer hunters. All we did was find a trail into the woods and stand around, waiting for a buck to walk by. Which none did.

I remember well the rifle that I used, a 45-70 Winchester carbine that Uncle Herb loaned to me. It weighed a ton. Uncle Herb called it his "punkin' shooter" because of the

"Minnows and Shotgun Shells"

size of the bullet it fired, a slug about the size of a man's thumb!

Today the old gun would be a collector's item.

Guns are one of the big changes that I've witnessed over the years. Today, by and large, deer hunters are well-equipped with well-made rifles, almost all with scopes.

Not so in my early years. Back then open sights were the rule, and guns tended to be on the cheaper side. Right after World War II ended, for example, a flood of surplus military rifles came on the market; German, Italian and Japanese.

Some were re-modelled into sporting rifles. But many were used just as they were made, some really weird looking stuff. All that was missing was the bayonet! It's good to see most of that junk now gone from the woods.

Clothing has also changed. And for the better. Gone are the red-and-black plaid coats and pants, replaced with good water-repellent blaze orange, which is both safer and warmer.

Gone are the old-time felt shoes and four-buckle overshoes, replaced now by insulated rubber-bottom "pac" boots that are lighter and more comfortable.

The laws have also changed. Back in 1948, Uncle Herb and I hunted on what was called the forked-buck law. Which meant that a deer to be legal had to have an antler with a fork at least an inch long.

To shoot antlerless deer was considered heresy. Today, it's recognized as a vital tool to manage the herd.

Which brings me to the biggest change of all... the number of deer. Today's herd far outnumbers the 1948 herd. Back then, deer hunting was limited to the North. Deer were only beginning to appear in central Wisconsin counties, and were unknown in the southern counties.

A Half-Century of Deer Hunts

Changes in habitat, sound management and increased law enforcement have been the reasons for the herd increase.

Over the years, there have been personal highs and lows... seasons when I was lucky enough to bag a buck, and seasons when I wasn't.

One of my high points was the mentoring of a son into a deer hunter. It's a challenging experience. One has to teach safety, respect for the laws, and woods skills. Yet when it all comes together, and a youngster bags his or her first deer, it's a rite of passage that is never forgotten.

There have been many other good memories... deer camps with their poker games and tall tales, snowstorms and bitter cold, good shots and misses, helping companions drag their deer, and they helping me.

And my best buck of all?

Well, the deer was only a modest six-pointer, nothing to brag about. What made it special, however, was the fact that I shot it on the last day of the 1963 season... while hunting alone... after my hunting partner had decided to call it quits for the season.

I'll never forget the sight of that critter down the barrel of my little 30-30 as it bounced along through the brush.

A deer doesn't necessarily have to be a trophy to be memorable.

November, 1998

Deer Seasons and Christmas Trees

Ever feel like you're a coin toss? Like you're a half-dollar spinning through the air, topsy-turvy... while the rest of the world stands by, saying, "Heads I win! Tails you lose!"

That's kind of the way the last week of November usually shapes up for me. The "heads" side of me is the deer season... the "tails" side is the Christmas tree harvesting season. And the two have a tendency to overlap, to even collide at times.

Not that I'm complaining! The situation is of my own creation, and I go into it with my eyes wide open. Yet, it's a juggling act, one that causes me to wonder at times if I've got both of my oars in the water.

Each year, the story's the same. Make plans for some hunting. Make plans for the trees. Then re-make the plans... and maybe, re-make them again.

Take this year, for instance.

My deer season plan called for spending the opening day on my faithful old deer stand out in the oak woods of our tree farm over in the Stone Lake back country, a stand where I've opened the season for the past 26 years.

There on a couple of boards nailed to the base of a clump of three scrawny maple trees, I'd sit and wait for a deer to come by. I'd gone out, checked the stand over. Everything was in fine shape, ready and waiting for my annual pilgrimage.

Enter the "tails" side of me. The day before the opener, one of our best tree customers calls. Could he come down the next day for a load of trees?

Well, of course, I said. As my wise old grandfather often told me back in my youth, business comes before pleasure! The trees would come first, hunting second.

But, needless to say, I started scratching my head, trying to figure out how I could compromise the two, to have the best of both worlds.

Well, I lucked out.

I'd move my hunt from my oak woods to the tree plantation, some ten miles distant. There, each summer as I work on the spruces, pines, and balsams, I see deer regularly. There, in a brushy corner, a couple of years ago, I'd even picked out a secondary deer stand.

Though the spot wasn't my first choice, under the circumstances, I'd give it a try the first morning. And when my Christmas tree friend arrived, I'd quit hunting to work with him.

Enter another factor that tends to compound the last week of November for me... the weather.

Those who were on their stands early on opening day will remember the snow that was falling. One of those fast-moving Alberta Clippers was moving through, dumping white stuff in dense curtains at times.

There I sat on my stand, gradually turning from blaze orange to white, wet, wiping the fog from my scope for the umpteenth time. And not a sign of a deer.

And when the 10 o'clock arrival time of my tree customer neared, I headed for the truck to meet him. Instinctively, however, I sensed that he might be late, and I called home on my truck phone.

"Minnows and Shotgun Shells"

Yes, he'd called. And yes, he'd be a couple hours late. And after a hot cup of coffee, back to my stand I headed.

Well, things finally started to go right for the day. The snow quit, I began to dry off, and I could see through my scope again.

And as fate would have it, after an hour or so wait, a fat doe stepped out of the spruces. One well-placed clean shot with Old Nail Driver, and I found myself tieing the hunter's choice tag that I was lucky enough to draw this year, to her ear.

And more good fortune. Hearing me shoot, three of my neighbors came by to have a look, strong young fellers who gave me a hand with getting the deer out to my truck.

And my tree customer? Yes, he did show up. And as darkness filtered softly down upon the tree farm, a load of our green darlings headed down the highway, destined to brighten homes for the Christmas holiday.

Which only goes to show that, though the best of life's plans often go astray, even the worst ones sometimes do work out.

It kind of depends on the toss of the coin.

December, 1997

Grandson's First Deer

The deer season is winding down, as I write. In a few days, a dusky silence will settle, like a curtain, over our woods and fields. And another season will be but a memory. It's been a good one. Lots of deer and many taken. Deer hunting is one sport where a person can't look back enviously at the "good old days." The good old days are right now.

We had three hunters in the family this year... this old geezer, who has looked down more than his share of gun barrels. Plus son and his son, our grandson. Two tags have been filled so far.

First, the old geezer's tale.

My deer hunting doesn't amount to much anymore. There was a time when I was as hard-nosed as anyone about the sport. I hunted hard, usually five or six days of the season.

But then, some thirty years ago, I bought some land and got into tree farming... pulpwood, sawlogs and Christmas trees. I soon learned that marketing of the Christmas trees collided with my deer hunting.

That's where things stand today.

Sure, there's some room for compromise. And I do. But my hunting is pretty much restricted to the first weekend. After that the trees dominate my time. Get a deer the first

"Minnows and Shotgun Shells"

Saturday or Sunday, or don't get one at all. That's what it boils down to. About half the time, I'm successful.

This season was one of my lucky years. For most of opening day I'd sat quietly on a couple of my stands, watching the gray dawn slowly change to pink as the sun began to peek over our popples. Overhead, several flocks of geese passed, yakking it up as they headed out to picked corn fields to feed. A ruffed grouse strutted casually past, only a few feet from my boots.

But no deer. With a herd of a million-and-a-half in the state, one would think there'd be no problem seeing one. Not true.

Late afternoon, however, things changed. Either three or four, I never could be sure, came sneaking, just flickers of gray-brown in the brush. And I resigned myself to letting them pass. No way would I shoot. But then, one stepped out into a narrow opening.

A good shot put the doe down in its tracks, and my season was over. No big deal. Just good venison for the grill this winter.

And that evening, I checked with son and grandson, who I knew were hunting on a second parcel of our tree farm.

That's when the season began to change to special. Special, because this was grandson's first year to hunt.

He'd turned 13 this past summer, and he'd signed up for, and completed, the hunter safety course. And in time, he and his dad had gone gun shopping. For a twelve-gauge shotgun, pump action. He'd use that with slugs this first season.

A month or so ago, a dandy stand had been built, one that dad could see from his own, where there'd be visual and voice contact, as the law requires.

I saw the stand during the grouse season as I'd walked the

Grandson's First Deer

trail where it's located. It's well-built with a nice flat floor, a little chair, and a railing along its sides. Just the right height for a young hunter to rest his elbow as he takes a bead on a deer.

Which is something I offered some advice on. Wait until you get a good chance, then take a good aim. Make that first shot count. That's what I told grandson.

And above all, make sure you put the safety back on after you shoot. Never walk or run with a gun with the safety off! Those were my final instructions!

"Yes, Grandpa, I'll do both," he assured me.

And the second morning of the season, he knocked down a nice nubbin buck! One shot, perfectly placed in the rib cage.

I talked to his dad about the whole thing.

"I'd heard a deer snort," he said. "And I glanced over at Kyle. I saw him raise his gun and aim. And I saw his shoulder recoil from the shot. Then he began to wave his arm for me to come over!"

And I talked to grandson, to get his side of the story. He's a modest guy, a young man of not many words.

"Dad came over," he said. "He was really happy, and he shook my hand!"

The words took me back some 32 seasons. To a snowy ridge along the Totogatic River northeast of Minong. To a day when another young hunter had shot his first buck.

Back to a time when I too had felt very proud.

Back to another special season.

December, 1999

Winter –

… *Yet as I headed home, my mind held a limit of good memories.*

Like the immense, almost overpowering silence that encompasses the Michigan wilderness this time of the year. Like the carpet of fresh snow that sparkled like billions of diamonds in the morning sunshine, and the cheery noon campfire on the shore that toasted our sandwiches and warmed our spirits. Like the big, bushy-tailed, black timber wolf that padded slowly across the ice to look us over, to see what or who was invading his domain.

Like the recollections of suppers rustled by a cook waddling around in longjohns. Like spicy bratwursts peeking from a bowl of steaming sauerkraut to soothe the appetite after a cold hard day on the ice…

Cottontails and Northern Pike

Early December is a time of change and adjustment for outdoor people in these parts. Hunting seasons, by and large, come to a close and fishing through the ice kicks in.

This year, my deer tag went unfilled. Which is not particularly unusual for me. Two days of hunting was all that I got in, what with the priorities demanded by the Christmas tree harvesting out at the tree farm.

Son, a far more dedicated hunter than I, did bag a deer, however. Thus, there's a promise of a package or two of ground venison or steak for Momma and me. Which is ample until next season when perhaps my luck will be better.

The transition that takes place for me from hunting to ice fishing wasn't quite so abrupt back in my boyhood days, as I recall. Back then, winter meant snow, and snow meant hunting for cottontail rabbits, a species of wildlife that was plentiful in the fields and woodlots of my farm neighborhood.

But I haven't hunted cottontails for years. The critter is not particularly common here in our far north, replaced instead by its first cousin, the snowshoe hare. I'm confident, however, that "rabbit huntin'," as we called the sport, is still popular in the southern part of Wisconsin.

Cottontails and Northern Pike

Rabbit hunting was good winter recreation for us country kids. Back in those 1930 to 1940 times, with little money in our pockets, hunting was a good way to spend our spare time and energy.

Just pick up a single-shot shotgun, a handful of shells, call the family dog, and you were in business. Farm dogs back then were multi-talented, all the way from putting the run on an ornery bull to sniffing out a bunny from a briar patch.

Rabbit hunting was also a great source of outdoor education. Done usually when snow was on the ground, the hunter had full opportunity to study what was going on in the wildlife world.

We country boys became quite proficient at deciphering the tracks and marks that were left by animals and birds. To this day, I enjoy pondering the messages I find written in the snow when I'm outdoors.

Cottontails were fine table fare too. None went to waste around our house. Just the other day a friend remarked that he'd sure enjoy a good meal of hasenpfeffer, obvious evidence that he too pursued the cottontail in his youth.

Gradually, however, as winter deepened, my thoughts would turn, as they do now, to ice fishing. About Christmas vacation time, I'd look forward to my Uncle Herb stopping by to invite me to join him for a day on a nearby lake.

Talk about sheer ecstasy! Into his green Pontiac with its wooden-spoked wheels, I'd climb. Most of the time, I'd be allowed to bring my gun along, a contingency plan in case the fish weren't biting and I could try for a cottontail in the cattail marshes that bordered the lake.

Across the ice, I'd follow Herb. A big man, he was an imposing sight as he trudged along clad in an old black overcoat and four-buckle overshoes.

"Minnows and Shotgun Shells"

And I'd watch as he'd chisel the holes in the ice, peering downward for the "pickerel weeds" that marked a good spot. There he'd set out a home-made tip-up, explaining as he did what he'd learned about the personality of the northern pike over his many years of ice fishing. Things like how to bait a hook with a shiner minnow or a dead smelt, and when to set the hook if a pike took the bait.

A lot of years have passed since those Uncle Herb days. Yet today I still look forward to the beginning of the ice fishing season.

This year it appears to be off to an excellent start. An unusually cold November put ice on the lakes early, and fishermen, though not I, have been out. Experienced anglers know that early ice usually provides good action. That seems to prove true for almost every species… walleyes, northerns, crappies and bluegills.

Thus, one season ends, and another begins.

Not that the shotgun has been completely retired. There's some grouse hunting left, and if the snow doesn't get too deep, it'll be tempting.

But you can bet that the tip-ups and jig poles will get a workout soon.

A mess of nice bluegill fillets would taste mighty good.

December, 1996

Pity The Poor Chaps

A bit of pity goes out from me to our dedicated ice fishermen. Those rugged chaps have taken a hit to the chin this year, I say. Here we are, going into January, and only recently has there been enough ice to fish safely.

Blame it on the mild November and December, of course.

Being a long-time member of that noble and honored fraternity, I've sympathized with my fellow brethren. I love my ice fishing. And over the 46 years I've lived here in northern Wisconsin, I've kept a keen eye on the sport.

Over those years, I reached a conclusion, namely that I could always find a place to fish through the ice by the first weekend in December. Many years, it was even earlier, like in deer season.

Sure I'd have to pick my spot... a sheltered bay, a protected shoreline, a shallow lake. But somewhere!

Not this year!

Not only did I not know of such a spot the first weekend, but also the second. And even the third weekend, almost Christmas, was slim pickins. And every experienced ice fisherman knows that December, especially early December, provides the best fishing of the season.

So my heart bleeds a bit for those rugged, drip-on-the-end-of-the-nose individuals, guys whose fingers are normally by now split, slit and bit. Split by cold water and cold wind. Slit by fishing lines jerked by hard-fighting northern pike. And bit by the sharp teeth of those fish as hooks are removed.

It's a grand sport!

I have to confess that my attention to the ice fishing scene was diverted somewhat. I was busy with other things during early December. Yet, deep inside, I know that, had there been ice, I'd have sneaked away for a late-afternoon try or two at the walleyes.

No way could I have resisted!

Finally, right after Christmas, I did go on my first outing. I tried Spooner Lake for northerns. Spooner normally freezes over early. It's a productive lake early on, but once the ice thickens and a snow cover builds, it slows down dramatically.

We'd had several nights of zero or below temperatures, and I figured there'd be plenty of ice.

Surprise!

I have my gaff hook's wooden handle calibrated so that I can hook the underside of the ice to measure its thickness. Five inches, I found! Barely enough to feel comfortable walking on!

A good number of fishermen were out, however... probably a couple dozen standing around watching their tip-ups or sitting on pickle pails jigging for panfish.

And the fish were cooperating. Every few minutes a flag would pop for someone, and the race would be on to the lucky line.

Ice fishermen are a sociable lot, I've found, and I talked with several who were having good luck on big sucker minnows. One young man had a dandy pike of about 30 inches,

Pity The Poor Chaps

which he estimated would weigh six pounds.

Myself, I used dead smelt, an old and reliable bait for me. Having never used dead bait for northerns, my new-found buddies were impressed with the action I got. I figured it was the oil in the smelt that was the secret, I told them.

Speaking of using dead bait for northerns, kindles some memories of my early ice-fishing days... back in the 1930's. Ice fishing wasn't too popular then. My Uncle Herb was an avid winter angler, however, and he'd take me along.

Living as we did near Lake Michigan, we got our bait from its waters. The shiner minnows we used, we seined by casting out a hoop net. Minnows, however, were hard to keep alive, what with the non-insulated buckets of the time.

Uncle Herb's favorite bait was a "bloater," a chub-like fish that he bought from commercial fishermen when they came in with their tugs after tending their nets. Unk had his own special way of threading his hook and line through the bloater so that it balanced life-like in the water. I watched him catch many a fine northern pike with those baits.

Without a doubt, our ice fishing season got off to a slow start this year. But conditions are improving. And, there's a lot of good winter left!

Years ago I had an ice fishing shack down on Shawano Lake. Over the door, I put a sign that read "Ice is Nice."

That's the way we hard-nosed ice fishermen think!

January, 1999

Bob & Butch . . . And a hunt from days gone by.

A Winter Grouse Hunt

Sometimes things work out OK even when they don't. Such was the case last week.

I'd gotten carried away by the nice winter weather we were having. Ice fishing was on my mind, for one thing. Conditions were excellent, and I gave the northern pike a try.

But the good weather got me thinking about other outdoor stuff. There'd be plenty of time for fishing. A whole winter lay ahead.

And it suddenly dawned on me that the ruffed grouse season was still open, through the end of December.

Now, needless to say, I had a poor grouse season this past fall. Not that there weren't birds around. There were. My problem came from the rainless October we had. It took a lot of pussy-footed walking in the dry, noisy woods to put a bird in the hunting coat.

But now, with a nice carpet of snow, maybe a guy could sneak up on one. The critters had to be around. Deer hunter after deer hunter had told me they'd flushed birds during the recent season.

The more I thought about the idea, the more I liked it. And there'd be other benefits. Both Butch, my German shortbrain pal, and I could use the exercise. Plus the fact that I could check the tree farm for wildlife, to see what kind of messages were being left in the snow.

And another brainstorm, a minor work project. One of the trails needed brushing. The popple, birches and alders were closing in, threatening to evict me from the property.

Anyone who owns a woods knows how much of a job it is to keep roads driveable. Make an opening in a forest, and immediately the trees try to close it. Mother Nature abhors a vacuum!

Why not combine the two? Spend an hour or two cutting brush, then do some grouse hunting.

That's what I did.

The brushing went smoothly. The power saw was sharp, ran well, and the chain didn't jump off the bar, which often happens when cutting small stuff. An hour or so of work, and my road looked good again. I was back in control!

And with that, I stuffed a couple of shells into my little twenty-gauge and turned Butch loose.

My strategy was to hunt the heavy cover, dense stands of second-growth aspen that have sprung up to replace the mature old-growth trees that we logged in past years. Surely there'd be a dumb grouse or two hiding amongst the bent-over ferns and thorny blackberry bushes.

I'd walk the old trails. Butch, he'd do the dirty work, that of checking out the heavy going, a job he enjoys to the fullest.

Slowly, quietly, I padded my way, the only sounds that of the crackle of a dead twig breaking, or the creak of the snow underfoot.

Butch was in unusually good form. The hunt must have been an unexpected treat for him, because he made the most of it, exploring every nook and cranny. Back and forth in front of me, he worked, bounding up banks and crashing

A Winter Grouse Hunt

down draws.

I watched in wonder. The guy's going to be 13 years old this month. They say a year of a dog's life is equal to seven of a human's. If that's true, then the cuss is the equivalent of 91! And no sign of slowing down!

Watch him, and I can read his mind. Every so often, he'll turn to look at me. "Hey, slowpoke!" he's thinking, "What's taking you so long? Get a move on!"

Long ago, I decided, that he's always believed that he takes me hunting... not the other way around!

And the grouse?

Well, we hunted some good ground. But not a bird did we flush. Not even a track in the fresh snow. The critters had moved out, probably into the stream bottoms where they can hide amongst the balsams and spruces.

So how does one find satisfaction in a hunt where nary a shot is fired?

I found it in watching an old dog work. In the obvious joy and glory he found in doing what he loves best to do. In the fun he had as he sniffed and snuffed in the upturned roots of wind-blown trees, testing the delicious smells of mice and chipmunks that lived there.

And I found it in the sound of his snoring, as he conked out, curled up, next to me on the truck seat on our way home.

He'd had a good day.

January, 2000

Ice Fishing With Katy

I had the honor of escorting a young lady to a "ball" over the holidays. A fishing ball, that is.

The outing had been born two summers ago. Back then, I'd taken Katy Edwards trout fishing. Katy is a very outdoor person. And she'd wanted to learn a few things about trout and trout streams.

So, with her in the lead, carefully following my suggestions as to where to cast, we'd worked our way up one of my favorite streams. She caught only a single trout that day. But she came away, I'm sure, with some good memories... things like the feel of a stream pushing aginst her boots, and the sound of the music of its tumbling rapids.

And out of the day came a decision. We'd get together for a day of ice fishing sometime, something else that she wanted to try.

Well, a plan didn't work out that winter of a year ago. But neither of us forgot. And this year things did.

She'd be home from college over Christmas, I learned from her dad. And she'd give me a call.

Well, as with most families during the holidays, we were both busy. It took three phone calls to settle on a date. Which narrowed down to New Years Day.

"Is that a good day?" I asked. "Maybe you're a football fan!"

"Katy Edwards loves the outdoors"

"Minnows and Shotgun Shells"

"That's what VCR's are for!" she replied. "I'd rather go fishing."

And at the appointed time, she pulled into my driveway in her Toyota pickup, clad in a warm down-filled jacket and felt-lined boots. I've learned over the years that one can tell a lot about a person's outdoor talents by the clothes they wear.

A half-hour later found me parking my truck on the frozen surface of one of my favorite northern pike lakes.

There's no better fish for ice-fishing fun than the northern pike, I've found. The northern is a fearless, voracious critter, one that bites more consistently than any other species. Want to show someone some winter fishing fun? Take him or her northern fishing, I say.

We'd set out tip-ups baited with smelt, which along with big minnows, are a good northern bait.

And as I began the chore of drilling holes, Katy was quick to lend a hand... skimming the holes, pulling the sled, carrying the bait bucket. Old fishermen appreciate that sort of thing, that quality of helpfulness and consideration.

With the lines in, we retreated to the comfort of the truck; out of the brisk, biting northeast wind that was blowing. And we talked.

She's in her first year now at the University of Wisconsin-Stevens Point, she told me. She's majoring in conservation, hoping to spend her years after college in a career of natural resources management.

She told of her courses, how she'd taken a forestry course where she'd learned to use a power saw to thin trees from a pine plantation. And how she'd been home for Thanksgiving to hunt deer.

"I had one chance," she said. "And I still can't understand how I missed!"

Ice Fishing With Katy

Join the club Katy, I thought to myself!

Late in the afternoon, the tip-up flags began to jump. And some coaching from me. Like how to position oneself to get a good hook-set on a running fish... and assurance that she wouldn't break the line.

During one short period, when the action was at its peak, the flags popped with regularity. No sooner would we get to talking back at the truck, and up one would fly.

"This is awesome," she said. "This is really great!"

Out in front of the truck, as quitting time approached, a bald eagle landed on the ice. We watched as it waddled about, penguin-like, on its stubby legs, pecking at bait fish that other fishermen had discarded.

And as we prepared to collect our gear, from the west a spectacular sunset crept slowly across the sky, painting the gathering dusk with crimson and gold.

A fair catch of northern pike went home with us that evening, to be filleted and de-boned... with Katy's help.

We'd had a good day, a special day... a ball!

January, 2000

Big Winnie's Perch

There's a stark realism hanging over the northern Minnesota wilderness these days... a solemnness that characterizes most of our north country this time of year, when winter continues to maintain its grip on the landscape.

Five of us, guys in my perch fishing gang, recently made one of our annual pilgrimages to the Deer River area, there to test our fishing skills on the several lakes that we've come to know the past dozen years.

A comment was passed by one of the guys that struck a chord with me. Why do we travel so far to fish, he asked, when we have so many lakes close to home?

His point is well-taken, of course. We do have fine fishing waters here in northwest Wisconsin. And anyone who knows me would agree that I spend my share of time on them.

There's a difference, however. And that's what keeps taking me back to Minnesota's north woods. It's that starkness and that solemnness that hangs over the country, especially now when Old Man Winter is still in control.

Drive the trails and roads, now virtually bare of traffic, and one can see nature's beauty at its best... forests of tall pine trees, frozen lakes, some so big that a person can barely see the far shore.

Not only can one see, but let the mind wander and ponder,

"Lunch time for perch fishermen (l-r) Dale Simonson, Joe Zanter and Al Spindler on Minnesota's Lake Winnibigoshish"

"Minnows and Shotgun Shells"

and one can also feel the magnitude of Mother Nature. Now, in winter, the landscape opens and a vastness that's not possible to appreciate in summer, when green foliage restricts vision, becomes apparent.

To some, the pine forests may appear lifeless. Crusted snowbanks cover the ground, half-burying the jack pines and popples that have died of old age and toppled before the wind. Yet life exists. With plants, the trees and shrubs, it's merely suspended... waiting for the warm breezes that will soon blow, to send their buds to bursting.

Of the ground-bound animals, many are asleep beneath the snow, waiting too for the warm breezes to send them forth.

And the birds, for those that don't migrate, all one has to do is look and listen. A grouse that flashes across the road as I drive. The high-pitched call of the pileated woodpecker back in the woods at camp. The throaty croaking of the ravens as they pass over Big Winnibigoshish, as I sit fishing its depths.

Without doubt, all of these values can be experienced close to home. But in the wildness of northern Minnesota, for me, they're magnified and amplified. And that is why I keep going back.

We had a good fishing trip.

Of our three-day stay, only one, the first when we caught a cold front passing through with its 20-mile-an-hour winds, was on the unpleasant side. But we hunkered in the lee sides of our trucks, and toughed it out.

The fish catching was on the marginal side. I had to work to tease the perch into biting, particularly the bigger keeper-size fish. That's pretty much the story of perch fishing all the time.

We fish with short glass or graphite rods equipped with

Big Winnie's Perch

lightweight open-faced reels loaded with four-pound monofilament line. The popular lure is the Swedish Pimple with the treble hook replaced with a single shank hook. Waxies and small minnows, cut in half, are used to dress the hook.

The rig is then slowly jigged just off the bottom of the lake.

Rod Keith, from Bruce, and one of the better perch fishermen around, introduced me to a new bait. Called a Power bait, it's a soft plastic worm-like lure. Using that in yellow on a blaze orange Pimple with a waxie covering the bare hook tip, I had good action.

And what would a fishing trip be without the amenities… Joe Zanter's elk steak sandwiches broiled to perfection at noon out on the ice. And the bull sessions and cribbage games back at camp.

Good memories such as those, and the awesome atmosphere of the northern Minnesota wilderness itself, are the reasons why I keep returning.

March, 1999

Hooked On A Hobby

Can a guy get hooked on a hobby? You bet! Especially when that hobby is collecting old fishing lures. Just ask Bob Essick.

I spent a pleasant afternoon recently with Essick at his Rice Lake home. There, the retired insurance agent showed me the collection of antique fishing plugs he's assembled. Not only did we talk about those old baits, but also about old boats, rods, reels and other paraphernalia that fishermen used years ago.

And with the whims of winter still bearing down, what Essick said generated a good case of spring fever in me. Just touching those old lures sent shivers up and down my casting arm.

Essick's been collecting lures since 1968. He's a longtime member of the National Fishing Lure Collectors Club. "I was the 22nd member to join," he said. "Now the membership is up to almost 4,000."

I asked him how he got started.

"My reason was a big muskie I'd raise once a week on the Chippewa Flowage," he answered. "He'd come up and look at my bait but never take it. I told some friends about the fish, and we dug out some old baits to try. The fish would show up, but never bite. I'm sure it died of old age!" Bob's interest in old baits had been stimulated, however.

Essick started fishing at an early age. Raised in Spooner, his dad would take him to Shell Lake. "My job was to row the boat," he told. "Dad used to fish with flies for walleyes when the mayfly hatch was on."

Today, Essick still enjoys his fishing and hunting, though some health problems have slowed him. "I can't take it like I used to," he said.

That love has been the driving force behind his hobby. Displayed in his den are many of the lures he's found. And more in beautiful wooden tackle boxes he's made of oak and birch to hold his prizes. "Changes in humidity will cause the baits' paint to crumble and deteriorate," he said. "So I built the tackle boxes to store them."

Like any collector, Essick has developed an instinct for finding old baits. He goes to garage sales, estate sales, flea markets and old bait shops. He talks with people who have old cabins on lakes. Garbage haulers are fertile sources. "Often when an old fisherman dies, his tackle box gets set out with the garbage to go to the dump," he says.

At the beginning, Essick collected any and all lures. But he soon found he didn't have room in his house and garage. He then concentrated on popular old-line brands: Heddon, Creek Chub, Pfluger, Shakespeare, South Bend and others. In time even that became too much, and he narrowed his collection to essentially one make, the Heddon 150 lure. Today, carefully displayed in trays in his tackle boxes, Essick has a magnificent array of 150's.

"They were made between 1904 and the mid 1920's," he said. "Some with elaborate scale patterns. Some are called 'crackle backs' because old Louis Heddon baked the baits in his wife's oven, and the paint cracked. People liked them, so

"Bob Essick collects antique fishing lures"

Hooked On A Hobby

he kept making them."

The old-line bait manufacturers took great pride in their products. The baits became a new art form. Essick in 1979 visited Heddon's plant at Dowagiac, Michigan. "The process was the same, only the materials had changed from the early days," he said. "Back then, they used wood, white cedar and southern gum. As many as eighteen coats of paint were sometimes applied. Today a plug like that would cost a small fortune."

Would those old baits catch fish today? "You bet," Bob replied. "Our old friend, the Pikie Minnow, is one of the best."

And today's more modern lures, like those made of balsa wood?

"They're great," Essick said. "When the Rapala first came out, the guides in Canada were renting them out at ten dollars a day, and you had to put down a deposit. The first time I used a Rapala, I caught my limit of walleyes on Shell Lake. You almost had to stand behind a tree if you had a Rapala on your line!"

We talked too about some of the old-timers he's met along the way. Men like Bob Ellis, a legendary muskie fisherman, who Essick said handcrafted beautiful baits. And Tom Newcomb, a guide and expert walleye fisherman.

And we reminisced about long-ago boats the old rowing guides used, Rhinelander and Manitowish models. "One pull of the oars, and you'd go thirty yards," Essick said. And early fishing reels made by two jeweler brothers; wood and split bamboo rods; and silk lines that had to be dried each night.

Nostalgia... I found it faintly etched on Bob Essick's old baits.

March, 1994

Crappies Shake Winter Doldrums

Mid-February, I've found over the years, is not the best of times for the dedicated ice-fisherman... years like this especially, when the snow drifts lie deep and stiff on our lakes, and the cold puts three feet of ice on their surfaces.

Sometimes we get lucky, and the winter's not too bad. Fishing conditions hold up fairly well. And what with four-wheel drives and power augers, we fishermen make do. I've seen late-Februarys that were ideal, the lakes practically snow-free, the days mild and sunny, times when the walleyes bit well.

Not this year. This year's been a frustration for us boys of winter. We've suffered through slush, bitter cold, icy winds, and of late, snow that has all but shut down travel on my favorite lakes.

I wasn't alone. The stress was showing on my pack of fishing partners too. Comments like: "Whad' ya hear? What's goin' on?"

My old pal, Al Spindler, called me twice for instance, the first time to try to organize a trip to Big Winnibigoshish in northern Minnesota, a perch rendezvous of ours. Resort operators plow roads as wide as highways on Big Winnie, and there are heated shacks that can be rented. But even with those amenities, the trip got frozen out. Forty below is no fun under any conditions.

A couple weeks later, we did get together, however. A weather forecast that promised some 40 degree temperatures (above, that is) prompted a call from Joe Weiss. He was off a few days from his job of flying airliners around the country. Would I like to run up to a lake he knew to test the walleyes?

I would, I replied, and how about inviting Spindler and Joe Zanter, another fishing sidekick, along?

Well, that's how it worked out. A bright, balmy afternoon found the four of us setting out tipups, after ferrying our equipment out with Weiss', ATV four-wheeler. Into the darkness of evening we sat on our pickle pails, patiently waiting for the flags to pop. Only one did, a bite that produced a plump five-pound northern pike for Zanter. No walleyes.

And on the way home, over supper, the talk returned to fishing. Anyone interested in trying again the next day, I asked. The excellent weather would continue, I noted. Neither Spindler or Zanter could make it, they said. But Weiss, he'd go. Where, he asked.

Well, from a dusty old fishing file stuffed deep in my brain came an idea. One of my old crappie lakes! One that I hadn't been on for several years.

"I don't know what to expect," I said to Weiss as we headed into the back country of Burnett County the next afternoon. "We're just going exploring."

In the bed of Joe's pickup rested his four-wheeler, my sled and an assortment of rods and gear. The ATV we wouldn't need, we found as we parked. An old snowmobile trail would make walking tolerable.

Twenty minutes of hiking and I began to line up my landmarks, criss-crossing imaginary lines to pin-point the spot I remembered. And with my new fast-cutting auger, I quickly

"Minnows and Shotgun Shells"

punched in a dozen holes.

The fun began immediately. Baiting one of my rods with a small minnow, I set the line a few feet off the bottom in the 25-foot-deep water. Barely had it settled, when the yellow bobber twitched, then began to sink. Up came a ten-inch crappie! A good start, but was it a fluke? Would the action continue?

It didn't take long to find out. Joe, too, was reeling up a fish. The crappies were there, and apparently they were hungry. By the time we each had our three lines in, a half-dozen keepers laid flopping in the snow.

The action was sporadic. A flurry of bites, then a wait. My theory is that the fish travel in schools, and when one passes, there'll be bites.

The fish averaged about ten inches in length. Not huge, but meaty. Not like on some lakes where you can hold them up to the sun and almost count their ribs. Three age classes apparently... the smallest, six to seven-inchers, we returned to the lake.

When quitting time came, a decent mess of crappies rested on a bank of snow; solid, cold-fleshed fish, the fillets of which would make good supper fare.

But best of all, we'd shaken the doldrums that an unkind winter had placed on our ice fishing season.

The day would be the start of better things to come.

February, 1996

Winter Logging Feeds Deer

From the seat in the cab of the big logging skidder, the scene was spectacular. All around me, in every direction, I could see deer. Some standing, some bedded down, others on the move, walking, sneaking through the woods.

I'd come to a logging job east of Lampson on the Washburn County Forest to look at two things. First, the timber harvesting that Dale Johnson, a young timber contractor from Minong, was doing. And secondly, to see first-hand the large herd of deer that has been feeding all winter on the tops and branches of the trees he's been cutting.

Johnson and I had walked a skidding trail back to where he and Lance Sohn had been working since last December.

"There weren't any deer tracks here then," he'd told me earlier. "But in a couple of weeks they were here. I'd guess there's about 150 of them now. We've found only six dead ones. The DNR looked at them and felt they'd frozen to death, rather than starved, because they were small late-born fawns.

"Just recently we've found one fresh wolf-kill," he added. "We've seen the wolf's track, just one animal that has moved in."

And as Johnson and I entered the cutover area, the woods became a veritable carpet of moving brown bodies, spooked

"Treetops and branches from timber cuttings benefit over-wintering deer"

Photo By Bill Thornley

Winter Logging Feeds Deer

by me, a stranger in their midst.

"I'll go back and get the skidder," Dale said. "You can jump in with me. We can get right up to them with that."

Earlier he'd told me how the deer had grown accustomed, even dependent, on the logging.

"They'd be there immediately when we felled a tree," he'd said. "Because the snow was so deep, we'd pull the trees, tops and all, out to a cleared area to work on them. Sometimes we'd pull a tree right out of a deer's mouth! Later I'd pull the tops back for them to feed on.

"They seem to like the white birch the best," he'd commented. "Then the maple and aspen... last the balsam. They browse it back to the size of a pencil."

And upon Johnson's arrival with the big John Deere grapple skidder, I climbed into the cab with him. There with him at the controls, some eight feet above the ground, we slowly eased our way through the cutover, approaching to within a hundred feet of deer.

The animals appeared to be in excellent shape; alert and wary, certainly not demonstrating the lethargy that deer on the brink of starvation do.

"We hope to be in here another two weeks," Johnson said. That time would carry the logging into the middle of March, when spring break-up would shut it down. Providing food for the deer until that date would be important, nutrition that would carry them until they could range freely.

Johnson said that two other logging jobs were going on within a mile or two of his own, timber harvests that were also supporting substantial numbers of deer.

And in that cutting, and the forest management work on which it is based, lies a story of how man can alter his environment, his ecosystem, to benefit not only himself, but also

"Minnows and Shotgun Shells"

the land and the wildlife that it supports.

I stood the other day on a frozen snow-flanked logging trail with Dale Johnson and Lance Sohn. And we talked about the mutual benefits of well-conducted timber harvesting.

The trees they were harvesting, the aspen and balsam fir in particular, were far overmature, they said, as evidenced by the rot in the centers of the logs. The harvesting of the old trees was obviously providing food for a large number of deer. But in addition, when summer comes, sun-loving aspen shoots will regenerate the area. Along with the young aspen will come a multitude of herbaceous plants, rich in protein, which will create excellent summer range for deer and other wildlife.

"Timber cutting benefits just about all species of wildlife," Lance Sohn said.

And people?

Well, the truckloads of logs that Johnson and Sohn have cut this past winter have gone to industries such as the Louisiana-Pacific Corporation, Hayward Wood Products, Buchman Lumber Company, Johnson Timber Corporation, Consolidated Papers Inc., Georgia-Pacific Corporation, and the Fraser Paper Corporation.

There the logs will be transformed into products for people: waferboard, dowels, lumber and paper. Not to mention paychecks for folks like Johnson and Sohn, and others who work in the plants.

People, wildlife, the land... all gaining in a win-win situation!

That's what I found the other day on Dale Johnson's logging job.

March, 1997

Fish Science Hall of Famer

In muskie fishing circles around Wisconsin, Art Oehmcke's known as "Mr. Muskie." I've known the guy for better than thirty years now, going back to the 1960's when I'd send him samples of scales I'd taken from muskies I'd caught; fish that he'd hatched from eggs, grown into fingerlings, and stocked in lakes I fished.

And now, at the age of eighty, he's being recognized for his 41 years as a trail blazer in the field of fish culture. Or should I say, management of that vast resource which exists in our lakes and streams.

Oehmcke is about to be enshrined in the Fish Culture Hall of Fame at Spearfish, South Dakota, an institution that honors people who have contributed mightily to the science of growing fish.

And it couldn't happen to a more deserving guy!

The Hall of Fame is an adjunct of a large fish hatchery operated at Spearfish by the U.S. Fish and Wildlife Service. That, in large measure, is what makes Oehmcke's award so special. He's been judged by his peers! In a letter confirming Oehmcke's induction, Arden J. Trandahl, regional director, states, "It is an honor to be recognized by other fishery workers."

Amen, I say! Judgment by one's associates is the ultimate

"Art Oehmcke has been enshrined into both the Fish Culture and Freshwater Fishing Halls of Fame"

Fish Science Hall of Fame

test of one's professional contributions.

Listening to Oehmcke talk about his career is a lesson in two things. One, how the profession of fish management has matured. And two, how natural resource policy has likewise evolved.

Oehmcke began his career in 1937 as a biologist with the Wisconsin Conservation Department, the forerunner of today's Department of Natural Resources. At the time, the state had a multitude of small fish hatcheries scattered across the state.

"We had both warm water and cold water facilities, all fed by natural water supplies," he said. "The warm water produced muskies, bass, walleyes and northern pike. The cold water produced trout; brook, brown, rainbow and lake. But the warm water species were all stocked as fry, and the trout as small fingerlings. As a result, the survival was very low."

Fish stocking in those early days was viewed as the secret to good fishing. Consequently, the stocking of millions of small fry-size fish was considered good public policy. "Stocking was the answer to everything in the early days," Oehmcke noted. "And the fish were stocked by popular demand. Whoever put the heat on got the fish."

From that beginning, he and other biologists set out to put not only the hatcheries on a more productive, scientific footing, but also the stocking of the fish they raised.

Oehmcke at the time was the supervisor of fish propagation for northeastern Wisconsin, stationed at Woodruff. "Can you imagine the public relations problems I had when I started to change all that! Businesses and resorts resisted. But fish stocking is only a single tool in fish management. It should be done only when there's a biological need," he said.

"Minnows and Shotgun Shells"

Today that premise is the foundation of DNR's fisheries program.

In the years that followed, Oehmcke pioneered many new techniques for the hatchery rearing of fish. Procedures like the successful use of ponds to raise fingerlings, temperature controls on water supplies to prevent mortality of newly-hatched fry, cross-breeding of muskies and northern pike to produce hybrid muskies, hatching sucker fry to feed the young muskies, and the successful use of commercial pellets as trout food.

Oehmcke spent 31 years directly involved with fish culture. Then he moved up to administrative posts in DNR, serving as assistant director of the fisheries bureau at Madison and district director of field programs at Eau Claire and Spooner. He retired in 1978. During his tenure he worked under five department heads: Harley MacKenzie, Ed Vanderwall, Ernie Swift, Les Voigt and Tony Earl.

Since retirement, he's worked as a consultant on lake management and hatchery projects. He recently served as an advisor for the new Spooner hatchery, the construction of which will begin this spring.

His election to the Fish Culture Hall of Fame at Spearfish is not his first such award, however. In 1982, he was enshrined into the National Freshwater Fishing Hall of Fame at Hayward. The plaque he then received reads, "Outstanding world achievement in the realm of fresh water fishing" and "For his development of countless fisheries programs."

"I had a lot of interesting years," he told me the other day.

We thank you for those, Art... most deeply... each and every one of us that's ever held a fish pole!

March, 1994

Putting Winter To Bed

Two seasons ended a week or so ago. I declared winter officially dead. And I put my ice fishing to bed for the year. Both seasons were excellent. Neither owed me anything, I told myself, as I closed the book on the two.

My decision began to shape on a recent warm sunny afternoon as I stood on the ice of my favorite crappie lake. I was overdressed, uncomfortable. And I peeled off a wool shirt, something I rarely do when I'm ice fishing.

That's when I first began to think that winter was over.

Coming to a final conclusion, however, isn't that easy. It takes more than one incident, more than just a sunny afternoon. Anyone living here in our north country knows that tomorrow may bring a blizzard.

But then a second clue, the haunting bugling of a sandhill crane passing overhead. And a bit later, the rapturous calling of a pair of Canada geese as they circled the shoreline.

The birds were returning! Surely a sign of spring!

And as I drove home, more evidence. There, slowly strolling through the roadside woods, was a skunk.

And the next morning, as I sat sipping my coffee and doing some backyard watching, another signal. Across the crusted remains of the snowbanks scampered a chipmunk.

That did it! Skunks and chipmunks are hibernators, and if

"Minnows and Shotgun Shells"

they were willing to call winter dead, so was I. Forget where the first day of spring landed on the calendar!

The decision was a good one. Now I drive highways flanked by brown, dead-grass shoulders, not by the mounds of dirty white stuff that the snowplows amassed over winter. And I cross bridges where rivers flow free once more.

Yep! Winter's over, I tell myself.

Another easy one it was! No deep snow. No prolonged cold snaps. No dragging on to the end of April. A winter that came in like a lamb, behaved like a lamb, and went out like a lamb.

And my second season, my ice fishing? Well, it need not have ended that sunny day out on my crappie lake.

I just chose to call it quits there and then. On a high note, with a couple of good friends and the fish biting.

I'd had a good season, no walleyes, but generally good northern pike fishing. And the panfish action, especially the bluegills, had been excellent. Factor in a liberal dose of decent weather, and it all made for good memories.

Like the last day on my crappie lake. Joe Weiss and Dave Jacobson and I had talked all winter about trying the little spring-fed lake. But the condition of its ice at times, made fishing it questionable. Last year, another mild winter, I never set foot on the lake.

The other day, however, the three of us gave it a try, picking our way around the open water that had already developed along the shore.

And we found the crappies at home. Nice fish, not large, just good eating size from 10 to 12 inches. Jacobson landed a nice one before Weiss had finished cutting holes for the three of us.

That's the way it went pretty much all afternoon. The fish

Putting Winter To Bed

were suspended off the bottom in 30 feet of water... where I usually find them. Crappies are fun because they bite like fish are supposed to bite. None of this peck-peck-peck, nibble-nibble-nibble of the perch and bluegills. Just drop a light hook baited with a small, lively minnow down the hole and wait for the bobber to disappear.

Then, it's set the hook and hand-over-hand the line until the fish flops out of the hole. Sometimes two of us had fish on at the same time.

Over the years, the lake's given me a ton of good memories, going back to the late 60's, when my old friend, Bill Waggoner, first took me there. And trips that followed with others... guys who caught crappies and had a good time.

Now, however, the time has come to dream about open water, of bringing Big Al, my boat, home and getting him spruced up for the summer.

The first-of-May fishing season opener will be here before I know it!

Big Al, I'm sure, will be rarin' to go!

March, 1999